Violent Conflict and the Transformation of Social Capital

Lessons from Cambodia, Rwanda, Guatemala, and Somalia

Nat J. Colletta
Michelle L. Cullen

The World Bank
Washington, D.C.

Library of Congress Cataloging-in-Publication Data has been applied for.

Contents

Tables

Figures

Acknowledgments

This monograph is based on literature reviews and on field studies conducted in Cambodia, Rwanda, Guatemala, and Somalia. The research project was designed and managed by the authors Nat J. Colletta, manager, Post-Conflict Unit (PCU), World Bank, and Michelle L. Cullen, postconflict consultant, PCU.

The Cambodian and Rwandan studies were part of a larger World Bank Social Capital Initiative (SCI) funded by the Danish government. Guidance was provided by Christiaan Grootaert, SCI task manager, and Thierry van Bastelaer, SCI coordinator.

The Cambodian research team was led by Veena Krishnamurthy under the auspices of Cambodian Social Services, which also prepared the final report for the study. Field researchers included Huon Sathea, Koy Pharin, Pho Seng Ban, Prak Somonea, and Ros Pheak. Special thanks are due to Liz and Toshi Kato, Ellen Minnotti, Janu Rao, Khy Sambo, Suon Sophiny, and Cheryl Urashima for their contributions.

The Rwandan literature review was conducted by Lindiro Kabirigi, Jean Rugagi Nizurugero, and Gérard Rutazibwa. Field research was carried out by Callixte Kayitaba, Anecto Hanyurvinfura Kayitare, Christine Kibiriti, and Speciose Mukandutiye. Elizabeth Acul, Antoinette Kamanzi, Therese Nibarere, and Anna Rutagengwaova provided organizational assistance. Toni Ntaganda Kayonga and Markus Kostner contributed valuable input and guidance throughout the study.

The Guatemalan and Somali studies were conducted by the Italian social research organization CERFE and were funded by the Italian government. The final report for those two studies was prepared by Andrea Declich, CERFE; Luciano d'Andrea, sociologist and scientific director, CERFE; and Giancarlo Quaranta, sociologist and president, CERFE. Their work incorporated theoretical and methodological material extrapolated from lectures given by Giancarlo Quaranta and Luciano d'Andrea at the School of Sociology and Human Sciences in Italy.

Fieldwork in Guatemala was conducted by Jorge Mario Martinez, anthropologist. Field research in Somalia was undertaken by Abdul Rahman Abdi Maalim, social scientist. Francesco Ambrogetti helped oversee the two studies and acted as a liaison between the Bank's Post-Conflict Unit and CERFE.

Findings from the four studies were discussed at a seminar on "The Depletion and Restoration of Social Capital in War-Torn Societies," funded by the Italian government and held in Almalfi, Italy, May 21–23, 1999. Maresa Berliri, head of CERFE's Seminars Department, and Chiara Giorgi of the Seminars Department organized the event. Among the participants who provided valuable insights on the four studies were Abdul Rahman Abdi Maalim; Alfonso Alfonsi, deputy general director, CERFE; Alessandra Cancedda, researcher, CERFE; Andrea Declich; Luciano d'Andrea; Volker Eichener, Bochum University; Anecto Hanyurvinfura Kayitare; Elke Koch Weser, University La Sapienza; Veena Krishnamurthy; Thomas P. Lindemann, rural institutions officer, Food and Agriculture Organization (FAO); Jorge Mario Martinez; Emma Porio, Department of Sociology, Ateneo de Manila University; Giancarlo Quaranta; Maria Noel Vaeza, senior adviser on reconstruction, United Nations Development Programme (UNDP), Guatemala; and Michael Woolcock, consultant, Development Economics Research Group (DECRG), World Bank.

We gratefully acknowledge the contributions of those mentioned above, and we especially thank Osman S. Ahmed, Patricia Cleves, Markus Kostner, Meas Nee, Peter Uvin, and Michael Woolcock for their insightful comments. Although the field studies were carried out by select research teams in each country, the basic study design and analysis have been shaped by the authors' experience over the past several years in promoting the social and economic reintegration of war-affected populations. We take sole responsibility for the analysis, findings, and recommendations presented in this monograph.

Finally, this work would have been impossible without the contributions of the many individual respondents who were willing and courageous enough to tell their stories about the human dimensions of violent conflict in their societies. We hope that this modest exploratory endeavor provokes further research, policy analysis, and programmatic action to enable war-wounded societies to heal and reknit the social fabric necessary for nurturing reconciliation and achieving enduring peace and development.

Part I
Introduction

1

Social Capital, Social Cohesion, and Violent Conflict: Background and Analytical Constructs

The Cold War, in which superpowers sought to maintain a global balance of power without resorting to nuclear arms, masked many local, intrastate conflicts by internationalizing them. What in actuality were civil wars among indigenes contending for local power were turned into "virtual" international conflicts fought by proxy. Externally financed economic growth and outside support for authoritarian regimes concealed deeply rooted internal ethnic, religious, social, and economic cleavages. With the end of the Cold War, this virtual bubble burst, leaving an unprecedented number of civil wars. Of the 108 violent conflicts between 1989 and 1998, 92 are considered to be intrastate (Wallensteen and Sollenberg 1996; Sollenberg 1998). Consequently, peacekeeping and peacebuilding have taken on new prominence as tasks for the United Nations. In the first 45 years of its existence, the UN spent 23 percent of its budget, or about US$3.6 billion, on peacekeeping. In the past 10 years this has increased dramatically; 77 percent of the UN budget (roughly US$12.1 billion per year) has been allocated to maintaining peace within rather than across national borders (Martin 1996a).

Unlike interstate conflict, which often mobilizes national unity and strengthens societal cohesiveness, violent conflict within a state weakens its social fabric. It divides the population by undermining interpersonal and communal trust, destroying the norms and values that underlie cooperation and collective ac-

3

tion for the common good, and increasing the likelihood of communal strife. This damage to a nation's social capital—the norms, values, and social relations that bond communities together, as well as the bridges between communal groups (civil society)[1] and the state—impedes the ability of either communal groups or the state to recover after hostilities cease. Even if other forms of capital are replenished, economic and social development will be hindered unless social capital stocks are restored.

A growing body of research has examined the phenomenon of social capital in an attempt to define the concept and the forms it may take and to describe how it may influence and improve the development process. Efforts have also been made to develop indicators for measuring social capital and to arrive at recommendations on how to encourage and support this dynamic. Few studies, however, have actually analyzed social capital and how it interacts with violent conflict—an important issue, considering the rise in the frequency of intrastate conflict and the importance of social capital to social and economic growth and development (Olson 1982; North 1990; Fedderke and Klitgaard 1998; Grootaert 1998; Rodrik 1999b; Collier and Hoeffler 1999). Such an understanding could enhance the abilities of international actors and policymakers to more effectively carry out peacebuilding—relief, reconstruction, reconciliation, and development.

In an effort to better understand the interactions between violent conflict and social capital, the authors, under the auspices of the Post-Conflict Unit, World Bank, undertook an exploratory investigation of four conflict-affected countries—Cambodia, Rwanda, Guatemala, and Somalia—and their changing social capital dynamics. The data for this monograph have been drawn from extensive literature reviews and from eight community-level studies conducted in the four countries. In a quasi-experimental study design, two communities were selected from each country—one that had experienced high-intensity conflict and one where the intensity of conflict was low. Despite the difficulty of the task, every effort was made to select matched pairs of communities, holding constant community size, ethnic mix, dominant mode of subsistence, and socioeconomic status. The findings are clearly limited by modifications in the methodology used in the different countries and by the uneven quality of data collection in each community. These differences were in part due to the differing capacities of the field research teams and the general difficulties in undertaking research in war-torn communities, especially on such socially and politically sensitive issues as communal trust, social relations, and civic and state perceptions and dynamics. An indication of the severity of the conflicts in these countries is that two, Cambodia and Rwanda, were officially declared cases of genocide (crimes against humanity) by the United Nations, and one (Guatemala) is considered by many observers to have constituted a genocide.

On the basis of the exploratory investigation, this monograph discusses changes in social capital resulting from violent conflict; the interaction between social capital, social cohesion, and violent conflict; and how civil society, governments, and international actors can nurture the social capital needed to strengthen social cohesion and so promote conflict prevention, rehabilitation, and reconciliation. Findings and recommendations from these four studies are preliminary, as each case study was conducted on an exploratory basis only. The study results are specific to the countries analyzed, although some broad generalizations may have wider validity. Further research is needed to confirm and solidify the results. (See the annex for a comparative summary of the methodologies employed and lessons for similar research in the future.)

The remainder of this chapter examines the concepts of social capital, social cohesion, and violent conflict that underlie the frameworks employed in the field studies and the subsequent analysis. Part II provides an overview of the community studies, including information on study backgrounds, historical perspectives, methodologies, and findings. Policy and practice recommendations emerging from the studies are presented in Part III. Through this process, we attempt to outline how societal cohesiveness can be strengthened through the accumulation of horizontal social capital (the nurturing of trust and civic engagement among like and diverse groups) and vertical social capital (relations between the state, market, and civil society) and how social capital can be a critical means for combating social fragmentation and violent conflict. We then posit what governments and international actors can do to help war-torn countries return to a path of reconciliation, reconstruction, and sustainable peace and development.

Social Capital: An Emerging Conceptual Framework

Categorizing and analyzing social capital is difficult, for there are many definitions of the term and what it encompasses. In general, social capital refers to systems that lead to or result from social and economic organization, such as worldviews, trust, reciprocity, informational and economic exchange, and informal and formal groups and associations. Although there is much contention over what interactions and types of organization constitute social capital, there is little disagreement about the role of social capital in facilitating collective action, economic growth, and development by complementing other forms of capital (Grootaert 1998).

Woolcock's (1998) model of social capital facilitates analysis across various levels by presenting a comprehensive framework that incorporates four dimensions of social capital: strong ties between family members and neighbors; weak ties with the outside community and between communities; formal institutions (including laws and norms); and state-community interactions.[2] The application of this model can help enable the direct targeting of external interventions toward specific dimensions of social capital—either nurturing and utilizing existing stocks or building new links that unite affected and disparate groups.

Strong ties (integration) form the primary building blocks of society, uniting nuclear and extended family members and neighbors. These relations, predominantly based on kinship, ethnicity, and religion, are largely protectionist, defense mechanisms that form a safety net for basic survival. (See Granovetter 1973 for the concept of strong and weak ties and Gittell and Vidal 1998 on the concept of bonding social capital.) *Weak ties (linkages)* are more networked and associational and connect people to the outside community. Examples are links within civic associations and networks. This dimension often bridges differences in kinship, ethnicity, and religion. These cross-cutting relations are often affiliated with offensive measures, such as civic engagement and economic enterprise, that give people the strategic advantage they need to move ahead.

Social capital is also expressed in more vertical, formal institutions at the macro level. This dimension of social capital (*organizational integrity*) encompasses state institutions and their effectiveness and ability to function, as well as the legal environment and social norms. The latter can include influential and potential mechanisms of social control such as the media. The degree of the state's integrity influences whether civil society complements (enhances) or substitutes for state services and functions.

State-community relations reflect how leaders and government institutions are engaged in and interact with the community (*synergy*). When an authoritarian state penetrates society, there is little space for healthy civic engagement or development of networks.

The definitions and indicators used in the four studies focused primarily on informal and local horizontal relationships, such as trust and cross-cutting networks, and to some extent on certain aspects of vertical relationships, particularly state and market penetration, as important factors in fueling conflict and influencing the formation and transformation of social capital. The Cambodia and Rwanda studies undertook balanced investigations of horizontal and vertical social capital. The Guatemala and Somalia studies tended to focus more on the vertical dimensions of social capital. The concepts and definitions of social capital used as a basis for the four country studies stem primarily from the works of Putnam, Coleman, Fukuyama, and Uphoff.

Putnam's seminal work on social capital elaborates on the nature of horizontal relations. Social capital consists of "the features of social organization, such as networks, norms, and trust, that facilitate coordination and cooperation for mutual benefit" (Putnam 1993: 36). Communities with positive economic development and effective governments are those supported by "networks of civil engagement," or citizenry linked by solidarity, integrity, and participation. These civic networks foster norms of reciprocity that reinforce sentiments of trust within a society and improve the effectiveness of communications and social

Table 1 Study definitions of social capital

Cambodia	Rwanda	Guatemala and Somalia
Putnam: "trust, norms, and networks"	Putnam: "trust, norms, and networks"	A complex set of factors and indexes was derived to enable the measurement of each concept: civil society, social responsibility, social initiative, and social capital.
Uphoff: structural and cognitive	Coleman: hierarchy and unequal power distribution of vertical associations; not necessarily mutually beneficial	
Grootaert: institutions and the relationships, attitudes, and values that govern interactions	Fukuyama: importance of trust, especially in relation to civic duty and exchange of information	
Measured as: • *Social cohesion*, regarded as the density and nature of organizations and networks (both vertical and horizontal) and members' levels of commitment and responsibility to these groups • *Trust*, with the propensity for co-operation and exchange (material, labor, ritualistic, and informational) as its proxy.	Measured as: • *Social cohesion*, regarded as the density and nature of organizations and networks (both vertical and horizontal) and members' levels of commitment and responsibility to these groups • *Trust*, with the propensity for co-operation and exchange (material, labor, ritualistic, and informational) as its proxy.	*Civil society*, that is, socially responsible actors, was considered the enabler of social capital. *Social capital* was represented by two autonomous dimensions: social responsibility and social initiative. *Social responsibility* was viewed as a self-defense mechanism of civil society that attempted to mitigate social and environmental risks (health crises, illiteracy, unemployment, lack of access to higher education, geographic isolation, conflicts, and so on). *Social initiative* encompassed efforts aimed at growth and expansion rather than at controlling risks.

Table 2 Study indicators of social capital

Cambodia	Rwanda	Guatemala and Somalia
Structural social capital represented by: • *Community events*—activities that increase levels of solidarity and collective action and build collective consciousness through shared actions such as weddings, funerals, and the like • *Informal networks*—loose structures united around a common shared purpose • *Associations*—formal networks with distinct form, structure, and rules whose identity and goals are commonly known • *Village leadership*—official (local administration), traditional (religious leaders or elders), or informal (people who command respect on account of their wealth or charisma) • *Links with external agencies*—village or commune ties with outside nongovernmental organizations (NGOs), church groups, and the national government.	Proxies for social capital: • Type, nature, and organization of *exchange* • Nature and organization of *assistance, mutual aid, and cooperation* • Channels and mechanisms for *informational exchange* • Existence and nature of *associations* and reason for their creation • *Intermarriage* and extended family relations • *Intercommunity relations* and mechanisms for *conflict resolution* • Availability and functioning of *infrastructure* • *Trust* • *Social protection* and welfare; collective responsibility.	Two dimensions made up social capital: *Social responsibility*—the ability of civil society to mitigate risks to the people. It was assumed that this capacity was higher under the following conditions: • Greater internal diversification in civil society • Greater number of actors within each type of group • Higher quality of the different collective actors. *Social initiative*—the potential of civil society to facilitate economic growth. It was assumed that this potential would be greater with: • Greater diversification and quality of the actors in civil society • Greater certainty that positive local factors (listed below) are at work • Less certainty that normative obstacles (listed below) exist. *Local factors* include confidence and trust; material opportunities (communications such as telephone service and mail; mobility, provided by roads and transportation systems; and services, including personal services, social and health services, and financial services); and cognitive capital, or qualified personnel with specific skills and know-how. *Normative obstacles* were defined as formal (for example, law), substantive, organizational and bureaucratic, social and cultural, and political obstacles.

organization. Trust, improved communications, and the flow of information enhance the efficiency of institutions (36–37). In this way, social capital is "a resource whose supply increases rather than decreases through use and which (as contrasted to physical capital) becomes depleted if not used" (37–38). Unlike conventional forms of capital, social capital is a public, not a private, good. According to the definitions in Woolcock's model, Putnam's work mainly refers to integration and linkages.

Coleman's (1988) definition of social capital is broader, including vertical associations that can be characterized by hierarchy and an unequal distribution of power among members. Consequently, social capital can be beneficial to some and useless or harmful to others, depending on its characteristics and application. Social capital "is not a single entity but a variety of different entities with two elements in common: that all consist of some aspect of social structures, and that they facilitate certain actions of actors—whether persons or corporate actors— within the structure. . . . Like other forms of capital, social capital is productive, making possible the achievement of certain ends that in its absence would not be possible" (S98). Coleman's work cuts across various dimensions of Woolcock's model, including integration, linkages, and, to a smaller extent, state and market synergy with the community.

Fukuyama (1995) sees trust within a society as a primary factor in its prosperity, inherent competitiveness, and tendency toward democracy. Trust, in his view, is a key measure of social capital and is accumulated through norms of reciprocity and successful cooperation in networks of civic engagement. It "arises when a community shares a set of moral values in such a way as to create expectations of regular and honest behavior" (153). Reciprocity, civic duty, and moral obligation are essential to a successful and stable society and are the behaviors that should emanate from a thriving civil society.

According to Uphoff (2000), social capital is "an accumulation of various types of social, psychological, cognitive, institutional, and related assets that increase the amount or probability of mutually beneficial cooperative behavior that is productive for others, not just one's self" (p. 216). Uphoff breaks social capital down into structural and cognitive components. *Structural social capital* refers to the relationships, networks, and associations or the institutional structures, both vertical and horizontal, that link members. Horizontal relationships are those that exist among equals or near equals; vertical relationships stem from hierarchical or unequal relations due to differences in power or resource bases. *Cognitive social capital* is the "driving force" behind these visible forms of social capital; it includes values, norms, civic responsibility, expected reciprocity, charity, altruism, and trust. All dimensions of Woolcock's paradigm are encompassed within Uphoff's definition of social capital.

Thus, Putnam's and Coleman's work emphasizes the horizontal and vertical aspects of social capital, while Fukuyama's work stresses the importance to the formation of social capital of trust—a grossly depleted commodity during warfare. Uphoff's work facilitates the analysis of social capital by separating its cognitive and structural aspects. To further deepen the analysis of the relationship between conflict and social capital, interactions at the macro level should also be considered. This broadening of the definition of social capital permits the inclusion of government, market, and development actors, which have a direct impact on the social capital environment facing actors at the local level, and helps identify measures to be included in policy and operational recommendations. The social capital dimensions closely affiliated with the macro environment (notions of organizational integrity and synergy) were briefly examined in the four case studies.

North (1990) and Olson (1982) define social capital to include not only trust, norms, and networks but also the sociopolitical environment that shapes norms and social structures. In addition to the largely informal and often local horizontal and hierarchical relationships in the concepts of Coleman and Putnam, this view encompasses more formalized institutional relationships and structures such as the government, the political regime, the market, the rule of law, the court system, and civil and political liberties (Grootaert 1998).

Narayan (1999) also emphasizes the importance of inclusion of the state in social capital analysis in her work examining the dynamics of complementarity and substitution. Narayan argues that the focus must be not only on civic engagement, ideally characterized by inclusive, cross-cutting ties that link unlike individuals and groups, but also on the effectiveness of the state. A strong civil society founded on cross-cutting ties that operates in a weak state environment substitutes for the state's inadequacies and hence is not a model case for growth. A high level of civic engagement, combined with a well-functioning state, complements the state's abilities and produces the fertile soil necessary for social and economic development.

Although the exact definition of social capital and the approaches taken to measure it varied slightly among the case studies, the paradigms of social capital employed in the four countries stemmed from the key concepts described above, mainly those related to integration and linkages. The approach used in Guatemala and Somalia differed somewhat from those employed in Cambodia and Rwanda, each of which also took a slightly different approach toward defining and measuring social capital. Table 1 describes the definitions of social capital employed, and Table 2 lists the indicators used by each study.

Violent Conflict and Its Interface with Social Capital and Social Cohesion

To better understand the emergence of violent conflict, the relationship between social capital and the cohesiveness of a society—expressed in the construct of social cohesion, or the nexus of vertical and horizontal social capital and the balance of bonding and bridging social capital—needs to be examined. As Berkman and Kawachi (2000) note, "Social capital forms a subset of the notion of social cohesion. Social cohesion refers to two broader intertwined features of society: (1) the absence of latent conflict whether in the form of income/wealth inequality, racial/ethnic tensions, disparities in political participation, or other forms of polarization and (2) the presence of strong social bonds—measured by levels of trust and norms of reciprocity, the abundance of associations that bridge social divisions (civic society), and the presence of institutions of conflict management, e.g., responsive democracy, an independent judiciary, and an independent media" (175).

Social cohesion is the key intervening variable between social capital and violent conflict. The greater the degree to which vertical linking and horizontal bridging social capital integrate, the more likely it is that the society will be cohesive and will thus possess the inclusive mechanisms necessary for mediating or managing conflict before it turns violent (see Figure 1). The weaker the social cohesion, the weaker will be the reinforcing channels of socialization (value formation) and social control (compliance mechanisms). Weak social cohesion increases the risk of social disorganization, fragmentation, and exclusion and the potential for violent conflict. Building community or social capacity is a key development task for strengthening overall social cohesion and the ability to manage and prevent conflict (see Sen 1999).

The work of Johan Galtung (1996) captures the intersection of vertical and horizontal social capital by describing the structure of violence as consisting of three basic social and economic phenomena: exclusion, inequality, and indignity. In many developing countries, unequal patterns of development, in terms of investment as well as access to its opportunities or fruits, have been a major source of societal cleavage. The process of globalization integrates markets and values, thus facilitating growth, yet it is also a source of increasing exclusion and marginalization, widening the gap between rich and poor within and among societies, and exacerbating the conditions that can give rise to violent conflict. The consequent exclusion and inequality have been compounded by the struggle for identity in a rapidly changing world: traditional values, roles, and institutions are constantly under assault as a result of the communications revolution and the penetration of markets and raising of expectations in even the remotest parts of the globe. The impact of market penetration has been intensified by the weakening of the state in the face of dwindling resources, endemic corruption, and the rise of civil society, which can complement the state's role but can also compete with it for legitimacy. As a consequence, wars are increasingly fought over control of resources and power by social groups within states rather than by states themselves.

Conflict resulting from exclusion, inequality, and indignity does not in itself necessarily lead to the eruption of widespread

Figure 1   Social cohesion: the integration of vertical linking and horizontal bridging social capital

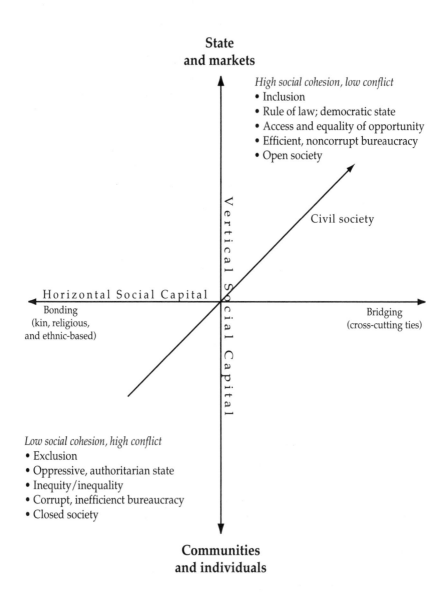

hostilities. The tolerance and coping capacities of the poor and marginalized are legend and manifold. Conflict does often engender large-scale violence if various structural conditions are present, such as authoritarian rule and a lack of political rights (as in Rwanda and Guatemala), state weakness and lack of institutional capacity to manage conflict (as in Somalia), and socioeconomic imbalances combined with inequity of opportunity and a weak civil society (as seen in Cambodia). The risk of an outbreak of violent conflict increases when these conditions exist concurrently or are exacerbated by other problems, such as the manipulation of ethnic or other differences (in religion, culture, and language), which can further fragment society and intensify the conflict (Carnegie Commission on Preventing Deadly Conflict 1997; Nathan 1998; Reno 1998; Collier and Hoeffler 1999; Berdal and Malone 2000).

Social capital can be readily perverted to undermine social cohesion and fragment society for individual and group gain, and this manipulation has the potential to lead to violent conflict. In Cambodia, the Angka (Khmer Rouge leaders) employed inclusionary social capital to strengthen the group's own resolve and weaken those outside the group. The Rwanda case illustrates that political and economic elites often use identity to mobilize and pervert extant social capital as a ready means of achieving their own ends. The Guatemala study reveals that groups and individuals suffer numerous indignities at the hands of oppressive, authoritarian regimes and a greed-driven elite that sets one group, be it religious, ethnic, or age-bounded, against another in pursuit of assets and power. Strong bonding social capital within Somalia fortifies clan allegiances, pitting clan against clan and impeding moves toward peace and reconciliation.

Within this complex matrix of factors underpinning violent conflict, two main features of social capital become increasingly relevant as potential kindling for the fire of hostility. Vertical relations plagued by inequality and an unequal distribution of power and opportunity (often accompanied by exclusion and indignity) can instigate violent conflict. The absence of horizontal relations—of cross-cutting ties between unlike groups in a multicultural society—can erupt into hostilities if one group is seen as monopolizing resources and power to the disadvantage of the others. And if, within these groups, high levels of bonding social capital link only like members, differences in access to resources and power may further aggravate relations and heighten tensions between those in control and those excluded. Thus, violent conflict is triggered by the presence of strong exclusionary bonds and disempowerment combined with a lack of horizontal bridging and vertical linking social capital.

The above precepts deepen our understanding of the root causes of conflict and illustrate how various forms of social capital, social cohesion, and violent conflict interface with several conditioning factors, such as inequality, indignity, exclusion, and poor governance. Although the community studies in each country touched on issues relating the above factors to violent conflict, the actual indicators used to assess violent conflict tended to correspond to violent conflict as manifested in social, economic, environmental, and political conditions. Such indicators as number of people killed, loss of access to markets, damage to biodiversity, and disregard for peace accords were used (directly or as proxies) to assess violent conflict rather than conflict per se, which may include intrahousehold contentions or common disputes over property or legal matters.

In all eight communities studied, violent conflict was viewed as both an independent and a dependent variable (a cause and an effect) in its relationship to social capital. That is, social capital can be constructive and support social cohesion and the mitigation of conflict, but it can also be perverted to hasten social fragmentation and the onset of violent conflict.

Part II
The Nexus between Violent Conflict, Social Capital, and Social Cohesion

2

Cambodia: State Absolutism, Alienation, and Social Capital

The aim of the Cambodian study was to assess how 20 years of violent conflict, which varied in intensity and mode, interacted with extant social capital. Throughout each phase of the conflict, the state targeted communities and individuals, virtually waging war against its own constituents while concurrently destroying the social foundations that traditionally serve as the girders for state building and cohesion. To compound matters, encroaching globalization, hastened by postwar interventions for reconstruction and rehabilitation, has had its own effect on social capital and has contributed to transforming the Cambodian social fabric.

Study Methodology

The Cambodian study, conducted by Social Services of Cambodia (SSC), included a literature review and six months of fieldwork. Field research staff consisted of an international research director and five local field staff (three men and two women). Because of the paucity of experienced researchers in Cambodia, field staff received extensive training in research methods and skills. Field research incorporated information from over 12 weeks of village stays and participant observation. During the fieldwork period, various research techniques were employed, such as participatory group exercises (village mapping, resource flow analysis, wealth ranking, and trends analysis) and semistructured interviews with individuals and groups. This approach to field research allowed good relationships to develop between staff and villagers, greatly contributing to the quantity and quality of the information obtained.

The SSC works in over 300 different villages in the Kompong Speu province of Cambodia, and from these villages 12 were randomly chosen as potential study sites. Comparisons of the villages according to various conflict indicators showed that all had been affected by the conflict. The two villages ultimately chosen, Prasath and Prey Koh, were the same size (populations of 651 and 654, respectively) but had different experiences of conflict. Prasath, the control village, experienced displacement only once, whereas Prey Koh villagers were displaced twice, and it seemed that more people had been killed there than in the control village. Prasath appeared to be a slightly poorer village than Prey Koh, adding another dimension of analysis.

In addition to village stays and participant observation, two household surveys were implemented, one to establish baseline socioeconomic information and a second to explore social capital issues. The baseline survey examined demographic details, landholdings, household occupations, and each household member's place of residence before and during the conflict period. The survey was implemented in all households in each village—130 households in Prasath and 114 in Prey Koh. Persons under age 15 make up about 43–44 percent of the population in each village; about 33 percent of the village populations is between the ages of 15 and 35, and about 23–24 percent is over 35. Most villagers in both Prasath and Prey Koh were born in their respective villages. Only a very small percentage of the population of either village could remember details of life during the preconflict period.

The survey targeting social capital issues was implemented in about 30 percent of all households (39 randomly selected households in Prasath and 34 in Prey Koh). The following *behavioral aspects of social capital* in the preconflict, conflict, and postconflict periods were examined:

- Problems in improving livelihood and economic activities
- Sources of information on livelihood and economic activities
- Borrowing and lending practices
- Ownership of and lending practices for livestock, household equipment, and tools
- Labor exchange
- Participation in groups and associations
- Availability and use of services
- Sources of assistance during crises
- Participation in activities for the common good
- Welfare of vulnerable individuals and families.

The *violent conflict indicators* used in the Cambodian study assessed the impact, intensity, and duration of the conflict (see Box 1). Cambodia's experience with violent conflict was manifold, as evidenced by the fact that Cambodian interviewees

---

Box 1   Indicators of violent conflict: Cambodia

Effects on the population
- Number of people killed
- Number of people physically disabled as a result of conflict
- Number of people mentally affected
- The extent to which violence is a way of life and is used to solve problems
- Number of family members enrolled in the army
- Number of people who left the village during fighting
- Changes in composition and size of the population

Physical damage
- Extent to which infrastructure (including houses, wells, roads, trees, and temples) was destroyed
- Physical traces of war (damaged buildings, craters, and so on)
- Area of land infested with mines
- Number of times village was relocated or dispersed

Nature of the conflict
- Duration of fighting in the village
- Types of group perpetrating the conflict

---

discerned different conflict eras. The period of conflict as defined for the study comprised three separate eras, distinguished by changes in leadership: Lon Nol, 1970–75; Khmer Rouge, 1975–79; and Heng Samrin, 1979–89.

Structural and Cognitive Social Capital

The definition of social capital used in the Cambodia study was based primarily on the work of Coleman, Putnam, and Uphoff. Horizontal and vertical aspects of social capital were studied, using a modified paradigm derived from Uphoff's work. Thus, structural aspects of social capital were emphasized, although inferences to underlying cognitive social capital were woven into the analysis when possible.

Social capital was measured within the study context by examining levels of *trust*, as evidenced by measures to secure livelihood and to engage in exchange (economic, informational, and so on), and of *social cohesion*, as indicated by collective action and the provision of social services and welfare. Social capital was broken down into various structural components:

- Community events
- Informal networks
- Associations
- Village leadership
- Links with external agencies.

As each structural component was examined, attempts were made to identify the cognitive social capital that buttressed these structural forms.

Community events are activities that increase feelings of solidarity, strengthen social cohesion, improve communication, provide a learning ground for coordinated activities, promote civic-mindedness and altruistic behavior, and, through shared experiences, help form a sense of collective consciousness. Weddings, funerals, and pagoda activities are classified as community events.

Informal networks are manifested in innumerable informal exchanges of information and resources within communities. The exchanges are for the most part spontaneous and unregulated and are the outcome of individual initiative and entrepreneurship. They are thought to be shaped by various factors within the communal environment, predominantly market forces, kinship, and affinity (natural bonds that exist between individuals who live close together or have shared interests and concerns). Rice-, water-, and plate-sharing groups are all examples of informal networks. On the positive side, informal networks represent efforts at cooperation, coordination, and mutual assistance and help maximize the utilization of available resources. They are highly valuable in providing individuals with support mechanisms in economic and social endeavors. These same informal networks, however, can be based on exploitative relationships in which gains are unevenly distributed. Informal networks can run horizontally or vertically.

Associations unite people, frequently from differing kin groups, who work together for a common purpose and have a visible identity. For the most part, these groups have clearly delineated structures, roles, and rules within which group members operate. Associations nurture efforts toward self-help, mutual help, solidarity, and cooperation. They are regarded as the building blocks of civil society and are usually horizontal. The main example of an association illustrated by the study was *provas dei*, exchange groups that trade goods and labor.

Village leadership includes official, traditional, and informal leaders. Official leaders include the communal chief and the local government administration. Traditional leaders are usually people who are revered for their religious or spiritual attributes (*achars*) or for their age, experience, and knowledge. Informal leaders wield influence because of their wealth, special skills, or charisma. Official and traditional leaders play key roles in the political, social, religious, and welfare activities of the village while shaping networks within the community and between the community and the outside world.

In this study, vertical social capital includes the relations and interactions between a community and its leaders and extends to wider relations between the village, the government, and the marketplace. The nature and quality of leadership in the community determine the level and quality of development in the village. To a lesser degree, unequal exchanges in resources or information establish patron-client relationships, adding another vertical dimension to village dynamics.

Virtually all *external links* with the villages are considered vertical. External community links include relations with the government, nongovernmental organizations (NGOs), and the private sector or marketplace.

State-Sponsored Warfare and Citizen Victimization

Thirty years of warfare all but destroyed most forms of social capital in Cambodia, yet the threads of violence predate the recent conflicts and are woven deep in the country's past. Since the fall of the kingdom of Angkor, political disruption and successive conflicts have plagued Cambodia. Relative stability was not achieved until the imposition of French rule, which began in the 1850s and ended with the country's independence in 1954 as a new constitutional monarchy. The kingdom of Cambodia, led by Premier Prince Norodom Sihanouk, experienced political stability and economic growth as the prince pushed for advances in health, education, and industry. Toward the end of the 1960s, however, the country began to destabilize as a result of economic difficulties, corruption, and the increasing threat of communism, and support for Sihanouk declined (Becker 1998).

In a coup d'état in 1970, General Lon Nol overthrew Prince Sihanouk, who fled to China, where he publicly formed an alliance with the communist Khmer Rouge. Lon Nol soldiers terrorized the countryside, splitting and destroying villages within combat zones. Concurrently, regional issues compounded the turbulence; the U.S.-Vietnam war spilled over into Cambodia, and a growing contingent of communists continually clashed with Lon Nol government soldiers. During the Lon Nol period, American planes repeatedly bombed Cambodian territory in an attempt to oust Vietnamese communists supposedly in the area. This campaign killed thousands of innocent citizens, destroyed numerous villages, and rendered much of the land unusable because of unexploded ordnance, chemical defoliation, and landmines (Ebihara, Morland, and Ledgerwood 1994; Nee 1995).

Lon Nol was subsequently ousted by the Khmer Rouge, which in April 1975 formed Democratic Kampuchea. Under the guise of communism, the Angka ("The Organization," the secretive group of Khmer Rouge leaders), headed by "Brother Number One," Pol Pot, initiated a radical agrarian revolution. This break with the past marked Year Zero, when many aspects of Cambodian life were figuratively and literally wiped clean. People were led from their homes in the cities into the countryside, where they and their rural counterparts were organized into work brigades and made to provide forced labor. Entire villages were dissolved and relocated; families lost their homes and possessions and were often separated and assigned to different camps. People who had lived in the cities and had been affiliated with the Lon Nol government or military were classified as "new" people, as were their families. The "new" people were treated much more severely than the "old" people—rural peasants and those who had fallen under the Khmer Rouge earlier. Fragmentation between "old" and "new" split not only neighboring communities but also villages and, at times, families, breaking both primary bonds of kinship and secondary bridges of association. The preferential treatment given to the "old" people created much resentment, although both groups generally lived under unbearable conditions—overworked, underfed, and terrorized on a daily basis. Meanwhile, opposition to the Khmer Rouge was forbidden; dissidents were tortured or put to death. The four years of totalitarian Khmer Rouge rule resulted in the genocide of roughly 2 million Cambodians, who died from political killings, overwork, starvation, and disease (Bit 1991; Nee 1995; van de Put 1997). Any remnant of vertical social capital between the state and civil society was shattered in the wake of a perverse accumulation and use of social capital formed by select communist intellectuals and a vanguard of unemployed, uneducated youth, pitted against the urban educated, professional, and business segments of society and the older traditional peasantry.

Vietnamese troops overcame the Khmer Rouge and formed the People's Republic of Kampuchea in January 1979. The new Vietnamese-influenced government, which was seen as a continuation of external domination over Cambodians and of the regional geopolitics of the U.S.-Vietnam war, continued to fight the Khmer Rouge throughout the next decade, perpetuating instability throughout the country. Despite this insecurity, during the 10 years of Vietnamese rule (the Heng Samrin period), recovery gradually began as conflict and insecurity waned. Progress remained slow, however, and was further hampered by noncommunist governments worldwide that were wary of the Vietnamese occupiers and kept Cambodia in relative isolation (Chandler 1992; Nee 1995).

With the Vietnamese withdrawal in 1989, the country was renamed Cambodia. Prince Sihanouk returned, after 13 years of self-imposed exile. A transitional government was established until the Paris Agreements in October 1991 that temporarily formalized the government structure. The United Nations Transitional Authority in Cambodia (UNTAC) oversaw the peace process, reconstruction, and rehabilitation, with mixed results (Ebihara, Morland, and Ledgerwood 1994). Elections were finally held in 1993, instituting a new coalition government headed by Prince Norodom Ranarridh, with Hun Sen as copremier. In 1997 an attempted coup disrupted the dual government, leading to a strengthening of Hun Sen's control. The July 1998 elections left Hun Sen in command of the recovering state.

Social Capital, Social Cohesion, and the Legacies of Violent Conflict

During the Lon Nol regime, traditional sources of social capital were severely eroded throughout Cambodia. (See Box 2 for an example of the interrelations of culture and social capital in traditional Cambodian society.) Many villages were forced to relocate or were split as a result of warfare, bombings, and Lon Nol recruitment. Within villages, exchange slowed, and solidarity around the temple dissolved. Some families did manage to stay intact despite massive dislocation (Nee 1995).

The Khmer Rouge ushered in another era of organized violence that included systematic attacks on traditional Cambodian society—on norms, culture, religion, organizations, networks, and even the family. Community and family members were encouraged to spy on and report on each other, destroying trust and planting the seeds of deeply rooted fear. A war against class distinctions was waged, as attempts to level economic status were

Box 2 Buddhism, Cambodian culture, and social capital

For the most part, Khmer village life has lacked traditional, indigenous groups and networks except those based on kinship or organized around the pagoda (Ebihara, Morland, and Ledgerwood 1994; Cambodia 1999). The nature of Buddhism and traditional Cambodian cultural practices contributed to the dearth of intercommunity social capital and to some extent facilitated the emergence of the brutal Lon Nol and Pol Pot regimes.

Buddhism stresses individual behavior as the means to personal salvation and does not foster a strong sense of collective social responsibility. It does, however, link Cambodians by creating a strong sense of national identity and by serving as one of the basic institutions of society. In many rural areas of Cambodia, the pagoda (wat, or temple) is a prominent feature of community organization and is the only bonding element of social life outside the family. Yet regular contacts with the pagoda, in the past as today, did not necessarily build networks of solidarity. Social capital in Cambodia has been essentially centered on primary links within the nuclear and extended families.

The strong presence of the state and the rigidity of the Cambodian political system have also influenced the development of social capital. Roughly 80 percent of Cambodians are farmers and live in rural areas. According to Buddhist beliefs and Cambodian traditions, their "low status" is the result of the merits of their past lives. This situation is unlikely to change, for the same explanation holds for the position of the rich and powerful. These beliefs reinforced the political status quo and to some extent helped justify social inequality and injustice. Politics was the domain of royalty, not farmers. If rulers abused their power, they were destined to suffer in the next life—it was not up to the people to take corrective action. Consequently, people tended to follow rulers without question, trusted in them wholeheartedly, and considered them almost divine. This is one reason why many placed trust in Lon Nol soon after he took power, despite the means he used to achieve leadership, and why so many were willing to follow the Khmer Rouge soldiers into the countryside without much resistance (Chandler 1992).

instituted by making everyone an unpaid agricultural laborer. By destroying all social, political, and economic institutions in this extreme communistic experiment, the brutal Khmer Rouge regime transformed and depleted what little social capital had remained from the Lon Nol period (Bit 1991; Nee 1995).

After a decade of destruction, forms of social capital gradually began to reemerge during the Heng Samrin period. This occurred despite the turmoil that continued to fester until the end of Vietnamese rule, marked by skirmishes between the guerrillas and invading troops, internal migration, and a disruption of agriculture that resulted in widespread famine. The Khmer Rouge had used collectivization as a strategy for transforming the economy and had broken up families to work in cooperatives. Vietnamese efforts to rebuild Cambodia in the early 1980s similarly focused on collectivist cooperatives, such as the solidarity group *krom Samaki*, which forbade private ownership and encouraged development through communal efforts. Although some progress and recovery occurred under the Heng Samrin government, when it did end, Cambodians welcomed the change.

Conflict affected social capital in Cambodia in many ways. Some of these were:

- The loss of human life
- The destruction of physical infrastructure, both public and private
- The disruption of services
- Increased antagonism and distrust toward the state
- Massive changes in the economy, including changes in ownership of property
- Population displacement (increased mobility)
- The breakdown of social institutions such as the family and religion
- Poor security; breakdown of law and order
- Extreme physical hardship and psychological trauma.

Postconflict forms of structural social capital and its composition do not differ greatly from those that existed before the wars. In both of the villages studied, community events, particularly pagoda activities and religious ceremonies, mirror practices of the period before the conflict. Nor are there prominent differences in how village meetings are held.

Informal networks continue to be organized by kinship and affinity, just as before the fighting erupted, but they are increasingly beginning to be shaped by market forces. Nonfarm activities, particularly small business and trade, are promoting new networks that go beyond the circle of relatives and friends. These have increased the need for mobility and information, putting people in touch with the world outside their villages. Networks formally based on the concept of mutual aid are giving way to new networks based on rigid reciprocity and the need to earn cash income, as is evident in the decrease of *provas dei*. Thus, informal networks are not dissolving as a result of the ravages of violent conflict but are changing in composition in response to the power and permeating influence of external market forces.

Associations sponsored by the government or initiated by village leaders and the pagoda show no visible changes from the preconflict period, nor do local associational initiatives such as rice banks, funeral associations, and water-users' groups. Of the two study villages, Prey Koh exhibits more associational activity than does Prasath, primarily because of its higher level of economic activity and energy. Prey Koh suffered more from conflict than did its counterpart, yet, despite the deeper schism between "old" and "new" people and the consequent more prominent threat of the breakdown of trust among villagers, associational activity increased. This suggests that the conflict did not necessarily diminish the willingness of people to work together.[3]

There is little difference between the type, roles, and nature of preconflict and present *village leadership* (including traditional, informal, and official leaders). In general, the role of village leaders in Prey Koh is more visible than in Prasath, primarily because Prey Koh has more resources and better links with the outside world, giving leaders more responsibilities. Prasath, with its small resource base, has poor links with the outside world, and village leaders, preoccupied with problems within their own households, are less active. Pagoda activities are more or less at the same level in both villages, and elders and *achars* appear to be equally active in both.

Various factors seemed to support the revival of social capital, including:

- Resilience—an inner strength that allows people to continue to cope and to rebuild their lives
- A strong drive toward self-help
- The powerful role played by the pagoda and Buddhist traditions in shaping the identity of people, and the need to reestablish this identity
- The need to restore basic village infrastructure that had been destroyed
- The knowledge that the government would not be able to provide what was needed.

It should be noted that some of the revival and restoration took place within the conflict period (under Heng Samrin rule) and has continued since then in the villages.

In the preconflict period, no agencies other than the government operated in the two villages. Government-provided services and resources were very basic but may have been of better quality before the conflict than they are now, particularly in education and health. In both communities, *state penetration* is still weak, and the substitutional effects of emerging civil societies, particularly in the provision of basic services, are only beginning to emerge. *NGO* involvement in village development and in providing services is a relatively new phenomenon that began in the Heng Samrin period. The conflict in Cambodia has resulted in a highly visible and active role for NGOs, particularly international bodies, although in the study villages their role has been intermittent. A more recent phenomenon has been the increasing involvement of the *business community,* especially in Prey Koh. Businesses there are clearly driven by the profit motive and are highly exploitative of the environment and villagers. At present, the development of links with external agencies in both villages largely depends on initiatives from outside.

The survey results revealed mixed findings about the relations between social capital and violent conflict (see Table 3). Primary-group relations of a familial nature endured during conflict (except during Khmer Rouge rule), serving as a defensive form of social capital and providing an indigenous, survival-oriented safety net. In contrast, secondary-group associations—linkages to market penetration and outward-looking, "offensive" forms

Table 3 Interactions between violent conflict and social capital: Cambodia

	High-conflict period	Low-conflict period
High social capital	Strength of vertical social capital: Many villagers joined the Lon Nol army in the belief that it represented the next government, thus proactively showing allegiance to the probable new rule. Cambodians put up little resistance against the Khmer Rouge when being led into the countryside. Bonding social capital within the Khmer Rouge and the Angka allowed those groups to flourish and maintain control.	For the most part, conflict did not change the structure of social capital in Prasath or Prey Koh but suppressed it. Most structural components have remained the same: • Community events such as weddings, funerals, and pagoda activities • Informal networks such as water- and rice-sharing groups • Associations, including exchange groups such as *provas dei*, which trade goods and labor • Village leadership: religious, traditional, and official • External links: government and, since the war, NGOs and businesses. There has been more associational activity in Prey Koh than in Prasath, due to higher levels of economic activity. Thus, conflict does not seem to be a major factor in this evolution, since Prasath was less affected by the conflict.
Low social capital	The Lon Nol regime divided communities by sometimes forcing recruitment. The Khmer Rouge did its best to eliminate all forms of tradition, religion, norms, family, and organization. All structures of Cambodian life were attacked. Villagers were pitted against each other and families were split as the state waged war against its people.	Informal networks are shaped more by market forces than by kinship and affinity. Old networks based on mutual help are being replaced by new ones based on rigid reciprocity and the need to earn cash income. Nonfarm activities are promoting new networks that go beyond the extended family and friends. The changes from integrative ties among primary groups (familial relations) to linkages that are more network-oriented (associational relations) are perceived by villagers as a diminution of social capital (defined more as kin bonds) within the village and as a result of increased market penetration.

of social capital that are more developmental than protective in nature—were stunted during warfare.

As the conflict waned, integrative primary-group relations were supplanted by secondary-group linkages, which increased in intensity and number. Despite Prey Koh's greater exposure to conflict, its proximity to market-penetrating forces transformed and strengthened certain dimensions of social capital in the postconflict period, mainly the more development-oriented dimensions. Prasath, still isolated, is marginalized from market penetration, and social capital has remained encapsulated in an inward-looking set of kin-oriented social relations. The research team posited that Prey Koh, which is closer to the highway, has easier access to market activities. By contrast, Prasath is located near the hills and until recently has been plagued by sporadic violence from Khmer Rouge attacks. The implication is that although violent conflict often shapes social capital in favor of primary bonding relations and an inward-looking orientation toward survival in the short-term emergency period, postconflict market penetration may easily reverse this pattern and lead to more outward-looking, associational social capital in the medium- to longer-term transition to peace.

The Cambodia case illustrates the ebb and flow of horizontal social capital, depending on the relative penetration of the state and market forces as instruments of vertical social capital. Vertical cohesiveness in the past has been promoted by the state and has depended on the symbolic leadership of the king. The succeeding line of oppressive, socially fragmenting regimes often perverted extant social capital. Although bonds of kinship remain strong, bridging social capital is now only slowly emerging and is doing so in large part in response to market forces. The integration of strong bridging horizontal and integrating vertical social capital to shape a cohesive society remains a challenge to Cambodia on the road to sustainable peace and economic development. Clearly, the future milestones on that road include the strengthening of civil society, the opening up of dialogue between the state and civil society, and progress toward an increasingly free press, a transparent rule of law (perhaps through the proposed war crimes tribunal), the promotion of local elections, and a more inclusive, participatory development process.

3

Rwanda: Hate, Fear, and the Decay of Social Relations

Although Rwanda seemed to become unglued instantaneously in April 1994 with the eruption of genocide, the progressive weakening of bridging social relations between Tutsi and Hutu and the increasing penetration of the state into communal affairs had been going on for decades. In an attempt to better understand the conflict and its interactions with social relations and norms, the Rwanda case study examined how social capital interacted with conflict in terms both of the unraveling of social fabric and the strengthening of social dynamics among Hutu that enabled the genocide. Although problematic vertical and horizontal relations within Rwanda led to the civil war, external factors, such as international interventions and changes brought about by modernization, also affected social capital stocks.

Study Methodology

The Rwandan study was implemented by local consultants and entailed both field and desk research. The first phase of the study, the literature review, assessed pertinent historical information and outlined traditional forms of Rwandan social capital. Field research in the selected communities was conducted by two teams, each consisting of one man and one woman, and included a three-week period of participant observation, six weeks of survey implementation, and three weeks of interviews with associations, focus groups, and key informants in the two communes selected.

The communes chosen for the evaluation were Giti, the control site, which experienced low levels of violence and did not feel the full impact of the genocide, owing to its own unique leadership and history of communal cooperation, and Shyanda, the variable site, which experienced high levels of organized killing. Both communes are of relatively comparable size: Giti's population is 48,000, and Shyanda's is 39,000. They share the same language, religion, and culture and have similar socioeconomic status and modes of subsistence, although Giti has been and is marginally more prosperous. Intermarriage between Hutu and Tutsi was and remains common in both areas.

As in Cambodia, surveys were implemented at the household level, targeting 1.5 percent of randomly selected households in three sectors of each commune. Each household contained, on average, five people. In Giti, 114 surveys were conducted and in Shyanda, 144. Focus groups of 5 to 15 participants were largely made up of widows, orphans, politicians, intellectuals, associations, business people, and mixed groups. Key informants were chosen from the target groups. Question and issue guides for both group and individual interviews were derived from the initial survey findings.

Throughout the study, difficulties emerged because of the sensitivity of the topic and the recentness of the war. Unlike Cambodia, where much time had passed since the genocide and few people were still around who could provide intimate details, the Rwandan genocide was fresh in peoples' minds, and the unsettling presence of *génocidaires* among the victims lent an aura of fear and intimidation. The research teams therefore made efforts to spend more time than originally scheduled in each commune to build relations, trust, and acceptance with residents. After the field teams strengthened their relations with communal members, discussions broadened to encompass details of the respondents' conflict experiences.

Social Cohesion, Trust, and Violent Conflict

The original goal of the Rwandan social capital study was to assess how conflict depleted social capital and how social capital was restored following the end of the war. After the initial findings from the field were submitted, however, it became evident that conflict did not necessarily deplete stocks of social capital but instead transformed them and that new forms of social capital emerged during periods of conflict. The study was therefore broadened to encompass these various types of transformations and social capital dynamics, which were examined by assessing changes in levels of social cohesion and trust.

Social cohesion was measured by the density and nature of organizations and networks (both vertical and horizontal) and by members' sense of commitment and responsibility to these groups. The propensity for cooperation and exchange (material, labor, ritualistic, and informational) served as a proxy for *trust*. In addition, the study attempted to develop indicators and measures of both vertical and horizontal social capital that were specifically tailored for war-torn societies. Indicators for measuring social capital were based on social capital concepts as described by Putnam, Coleman, and Fukuyama and were adapted to the specificities of Rwandan society. Related measures examined as proxies for social cohesion and trust included:

- Channels and mechanisms for exchange of information
- Existence and nature of associations and the reason for their creation (whether based on shared interests or on prescribed commonality, such as familial relations)
- Intermarriage and extended family relations
- Intercommunity relations and mechanisms for conflict resolution
- Availability and functioning of infrastructure
- Types, nature, and organization of exchange and interdependence
- Nature and organization of assistance, mutual aid, and cooperation (including sharing of basic necessities such as water, firewood, and salt)
- Social protection and welfare; collective responsibility.

To confirm that these factors were considered representative of social capital not only by the researchers but also by those being interviewed, survey questions and focus group interviews sought to elicit what social capital meant to each participant. Throughout survey implementation and with each focus group, it became clear that participants and researchers had approximately the same definition of social capital. Although each focus group had its own interpretation, the combined concepts covered almost all facets of social capital as defined for the study. Participants in both communities viewed social capital as including mutual assistance, trust, solidarity, civic duty, collective action, protection of the vulnerable, peaceful cohabitation, and on a larger scale, a just political system engendered by the state.

Indicators of violent conflict in Rwanda included social, economic, environmental, and political factors (Box 3). Changes in social capital as a result of violent conflict were assessed over varying periods of time (that is, pre- and postconflict). During

---

Box 3   Indicators of violent conflict: Rwanda

Social factors
- Number of people killed
- Number of communities and families destroyed
- Number of people physically disabled as a result of fighting
- Number of people relocated

Economic factors
- Destruction of economic infrastructure
- Loss of access to markets
- Damage to resources necessary for production

Environmental factors
- Extent to which crops were lost and fields were destroyed
- Damage to biodiversity
- Area of land laid waste due to mass migration
- Area of land infested with mines

Political factors
- Disregard for peace accords
- Dissolution of government

the assessment, the period of conflict was defined solely by the interviewees, who equated it with the genocide of April–July 1994. It should be noted, however, that violence and conflict have plagued Rwanda for decades and that the civil war officially began in October 1990. Since the end of the genocide, widespread violence has continued, with revenge killings and civil war along Rwanda's borders and within the Democratic Republic of Congo (DRC, the former Zaire).

The Anatomy of a Genocide

The 1994 massacres killed more people more quickly than any other mass slaughter in recorded history—some 800,000 died within a three-month period at the hands of their brethren (Berkeley 1998). Historically, however, ethnic hatred, which fueled this armed eruption, did not exist between Hutu and Tutsi. During precolonial times, the two groups coexisted symbiotically, with complementary modes of subsistence (nomadic pastoralism and sedentary agriculture). They were neither similar nor equal. Distinctions between the groups stemmed from membership in different classes, not from dissimilar ethnic backgrounds. Being labeled Hutu or Tutsi simply meant belonging to a loosely defined category based on occupation or class; whereas the Hutu were cultivators, the Tutsi were pastoralists and generally belonged to the ruling and warrior classes. Most important, group membership was not static (Newbury 1988; Prunier 1997).

Relations between Hutu and Tutsi worsened under the Belgian colonial administration. By supporting minority Tutsi rule, colonization further entrenched socioeconomic disparities and solidified the divide between the groups along "ethnic" (rather than class) lines.[4] The arbitrary distinctions between the groups were sharpened by colonial mythology, which relegated the Hutu cultivators to a lower status and categorized the pastoral Tutsi as the superior ruling class. A census taken in 1926 forced Hutu and Tutsi to choose their "ethnic" identity. What had once been a dynamic system of classes became a static system based on "ethnicity," which later became a (much-abused) tool for manipulation of the masses by an elite ruling group (Lemarchand 1970; Newbury 1988; Prunier 1997).

In the early and mid-1950s, the colonial government, under pressure from the Catholic Church, gave the Hutu greater access to socioeconomic and political systems. The increasing liberties extended to the Hutu became a cause of concern to the ruling Tutsi, who, as a minority, feared an uprising by the majority. Ethnic politics intensified in 1959, and the Party for the Emancipation of the Hutu People (Parmehutu) ousted the Tutsi regime with the support of Belgian forces. Skirmishes between Hutu and Tutsi spread throughout Rwanda, killing thousands and forcing a massive Tutsi migration. The Hutu elite, which gained power in 1961 and retained it when the country became independent in 1962, began to focus on marginalizing the Tutsi minority. Traditional social and political systems such as the role of elders and the *gacaca* conflict-resolution mechanism were replaced by the central administration as the state penetrated ever deeper into the lives of the citizenry. Pastoral Tutsi cultural traditions were progressively banned, and exclusively "Hutu" traditions became more closely identified with Banyarwanda culture, which encompassed both Hutu and Tutsi aspects (Lemarchand 1970; Prunier 1997).

Soon after the Hutu extremists took power, Tutsi rebel groups based in Burundi, Tanzania, Uganda, and the DRC (then called Zaire) began targeting Hutu officials. Tutsi-led incursions into Rwanda initiated a cycle of violence, massacres, and Tutsi flight into neighboring countries. This tragic pattern continued over the next 30 years. The government became increasingly repressive against Tutsi, violating their rights and institutionally excluding them from educational and employment opportunities. Sinking commodity prices, increasing debt, and government corruption led President Juvenal Habyarimana's regime to deflect attention from the worsening economic crisis by fueling the flames of ethnic hatred (Prunier 1997).

Tutsi rebel forces of the Rwandese Patriotic Front (RPF) invaded northern Rwanda in October 1990, sparking increased insecurity and killings in the area. In response, Rwandan security forces distributed arms to local civilian officials, and the national army was expanded to roughly 50,000 men. Many Tutsi businessmen, teachers, and priests were arrested and were accused, on the basis of their ethnicity, of collaboration with the rebels even if they had no connection with them. The RPF continued its attacks within Rwanda's borders throughout 1991and 1992, exacerbating hate politics and violent rhetoric against Tutsi. At the same time, President Habyarimana took small steps toward liberalizing the political system, mainly in an effort to maintain his power, and the repression against the Tutsi lessened somewhat. More drastic steps to retain control were implemented in late 1992, when the Habyarimana regime began to train Hutu extremist militia groups known as the Interahamwe and the Impuzamugambi, while it paradoxically pursued peace talks with the rebel forces in 1993 and early 1994 (Prunier 1997; Uvin 1998).

On April 6, 1994, President Habyarimana's plane was shot down over Rwanda's capital, Kigali. Government forces and militia immediately began attacking Tutsi and moderate Hutu. Within the next three months, brutal killings of Tutsi erupted throughout the country. Although some Hutu willingly participated in the massacres, others were ordered or forced to kill. A campaign of Tutsi elimination ("clearing the countryside") targeted individuals, neighborhoods, and (by focusing on universities and hospitals) professions. Roughly 2 million refugees were forced to leave the country, and around 1 million people were internally displaced. During the genocide, Rwandan society collapsed completely: business and agricultural activities ceased, skilled people and the intelligentsia were slaughtered or fled, the infrastructure was purposefully destroyed, and government operations, including legal, educational, and health activities, completely dissolved (Des Forges 1999).

After the RPF forces took Kigali in July 1994, hundreds of thousands of Hutu fled to neighboring countries, many of them destroying everything in their path as they left. Refugee camps set up for these Hutu masses inadvertently supported the radical groups responsible for organizing and perpetrating the genocide (primarily, the Interahamwe). Meanwhile, Tutsi refugees, from both the 1994 tragedies and the 1959 flight, spilled back into Rwanda. Chaos ensued during this massive return, and much looting, pillaging, and squatting took place. As time passed, government attempts to repatriate Hutu refugees were unsuccessful, for many feared widespread reprisal killings.[5] Finally, in 1996, the RPF government grew impatient with the security threat within the bordering refugee camps and forced the return of refugees from neighboring Zaire. Soon afterward, over 1 million Hutu returned home from Burundi, Tanzania, Uganda, and Zaire (Prunier 1997).

Throughout the five years since the genocide, Interahamwe forces have kept united, mainly hiding on DRC territory. Their incursions into northwestern and southwestern Rwanda have kept these regions relatively unstable and caused them to lag in development. The March 1999 local elections were a major step forward for the government, for they helped alleviate criticism of its legitimacy. Although Rwanda has made much progress since the war, many Rwandans are still haunted by its terror. Securing food and shelter has been difficult for many survivors. As a legacy of the genocide, homeless orphans wander the streets, and widows and wives of men in prison struggle to make ends meet. Widespread poverty and severely damaged infrastructure hamper growth and development. Despite all this, the Rwandan people in general seem to have hope for the future, but they worry about Interahamwe activities in the DRC and about the security of Rwandan areas along the border with that country (Prunier 1997; Gourevitch 1998).

The Perversion of Social Capital

During the genocide, social capital atrophied as the country, communities, and families fell prey to hatred and violence. Yet integrative forms of social capital increased within families fighting for survival, among individuals attempting to save or rescue Tutsi, and in the small Muslim community within Rwanda, which never took part in the genocide. Strong, exclusionary social capital also emerged within Hutu extremism, with extremely negative ramifications for those excluded—showing that violence can coexist with, or be the result of, strong bonding social capital among its perpetrators.[6]

As the formal Hutu government began to splinter, a primary operating unit emerged that coordinated the genocide. Communities split as orders calling for Hutu to kill Tutsi originated from the central government and were spread throughout Rwanda by way of local leaders, who helped mobilize the masses. Of the nearly 60 percent of the Rwandan population under age 20, few had hopes of obtaining land or jobs. This bleak reality facilitated the recruitment of Hutu and their acceptance of Tutsi hate propaganda. Once the killing began, Hutu killed not only Tutsi unknown to them but also their neighbors and, in some cases, even family members. These indiscriminate yet intimate killings led to the disintegration of communes and families and fragmented social cohesion in general. The violence to some extent also followed from the breakdown of societal structures brought about by earlier hate propaganda and ethnic strife. Although there were numerous Hutu who hid and saved Tutsi, many participated in the killings out of a sense of perceived ethnic duty, because of loyalty to the Hutu-controlled state, and in response to outright threats against their lives or their families' lives. To make matters more complex, some Tutsi with Hutu physical characteristics killed Tutsi to save themselves (Gourevitch 1998; Des Forges 1999).

In various ways, the genocide was a powerful communal-building exercise, at least among participating Hutu. Seeking to preserve their control and resources, Hutu Power groups achieved their ultimate success by mobilizing exclusionary and divisive social capital that bonded (primarily) unemployed, uneducated Hutu youth to form the Interahamwe. High levels of social capital existed both vertically and horizontally among Hutu ranks, while bridging social capital that linked Hutu with Tutsi was all but eliminated. Within Hutu extremism, state-driven vertical social capital fueled the success of communal-level Hutu groups through excellent information networks, reinvented past traditions, and a sense of solidarity, obligation, and civic duty (Prunier 1997). Social capital within the groups increased, as links between them waned, further splitting society. The bridging social capital that had existed, even though in a weak form, between diverse communal groups was now rapidly transformed into purely bonding social capital founded on fear and survival as Hutu and Tutsi groups coalesced on each side of the divide.

In the initial weeks of the genocide, precise lists of Tutsi and details of their residences helped expedite the killings and ensure thoroughness. The media were used to spread hate propaganda against Tutsi. For example, Radio et Télévision Libre des Mille Collines broadcast lists of Hutu in each commune who had not participated in the killings, publicly pressuring them to join the genocide. Such mass information networks kept the Interahamwe informed on who had been killed, who had not yet been removed, and who had helped facilitate the killing process. By spreading hate, fear, suspicion, and greed, the Hutu extremists were able to whip the Hutu masses into a murderous frenzy (Gourevitch 1998; Des Forges 1999).

Extremist Hutu also gained a following partly by invoking tradition. They appealed to precolonial Rwandan society and coopted existing value structures by reinventing traditions and applying them in a new way. For instance, the nomenclature used by extremist Hutu groups was similar to that of precolonial militias and blood brotherhoods. The propaganda utilized to fuel Hutu actions referred to traditional social capital in the form of cooperative labor (*umuganda*), which had evolved into forced labor and was seen as abusive to Hutu. The slogan of the 1959 massacres was renewed: *tugire gukora akazi*, "let us go and do the work" (Prunier 1997; Gourevitch 1998).

Génocidaires were united by the collective action of killing, which helped create feelings of collective consciousness, commonality, shared goals, and solidarity. For example, in Kinyarwanda, Interahamwe means "those who attach together," and Impuzamugambi means "single-minded ones" or "those who have the same goal." The manipulation of fear and hatred against Tutsi created solidarity among Hutu. For those who joined in the killings, the hate propaganda against Tutsi was attractive because it justified their actions and eased their consciences. Furthermore, mass participation in the killings made it tremendously difficult to assign guilt to individuals. In the words of a participant in the genocide, "no one person killed any one person" (Des Forges 1999: 770).

The success of the genocide depended in part on civilians' sense of civic duty and on the historical strength of the central government. Vertical social capital, manifested in almost absolute state power, had historically penetrated Rwandan society so deeply as to supersede horizontal relations or loyalties. Officials from the police, local administrations, and military forces went door to door requisitioning men to partake in their "national duty" of eliminating Tutsi, and Hutu voluntarily or begrudgingly followed these orders. Killing Tutsi was portrayed as a Hutu civic duty; such phrases as "do your work" or "it is your duty to help clear the field"—to eradicate the *inyenzi* (cockroaches), meaning Tutsi—were current. The image of killing as a means of self-defense against the RPF invasion was also employed, with the resounding urgency of "kill or be killed" (Prunier 1997).

Although this perverse manipulation of social capital made possible the mass recruitment of Hutu, real social and economic gains proved an added incentive for Hutu involvement. Population density in Rwanda had attained incredible heights; in Shyanda for instance, it had reached 668 people per square kilometer by 1989 (Prunier 1997). As land became scarcer, drought and poor crop prices compounded the economic crisis. Tutsi elimination would benefit the Hutu who participated in the killings by decreasing the number of competitors for land, homes, cattle, and other possessions.

Cooperation without Trust

Before the genocide, potential bridging social capital existed in the form of exchange, mutual assistance, and reciprocity. Typically, within Rwandan society there were five types of associative groups: cooperatives; farmers' organizations (smaller, less formal cooperatives); tontines (rotating savings and credit associations) and other informal associations; foreign and local development NGOs; and churches (Uvin 1998). Although these groups may have been numerous and widespread, the relations created by them were largely exclusionary and tended not to bridge group divides. This was especially true of NGOs supported by external aid. An opportunity to manage diversity and prevent violent conflict may have been missed as the economic ends of development overshadowed the social goals of strengthening social cohesion.

Many international efforts to support and encourage the growth of civil society in Rwanda were made in the 1980s and early 1990s, and many new organizations and NGOs appeared, thanks to these efforts. The mere existence of NGOs and other civil society organizations, however, does not necessarily promote democracy or pluralism, nor does it automatically form bridging social capital that links different groups. For the most part, NGOs in Rwanda were apolitical, service-oriented, and closely affiliated with the state. Moreover, there was not enough social or political space for civil society to truly flourish. As Uvin (1998) notes, extreme poverty, inequality, clientelism, and poor information networks, compounded by the social, economic, and political marginalization of the rural populace (the majority of Rwandans), made the emergence of an autonomous, highly developed civil society all but impossible. Thus, despite the abundance of these associative groups, the social capital present was not sufficiently inclusive to counterbalance the hate politics generated by Hutu extremists.

Since the end of the genocide, attempts have been made to place Hutu in government positions to balance political power, and space has been created for the reemergence of civil society actors. The new social fabric of Rwanda, however, is complicated, laden with subgroups and schisms. For example, there is the contentious issue of the resettlement of large numbers of returning Hutu and Tutsi. The latter are divided both by the duration of their stay abroad and by where they sought refuge. Those returning from Uganda are perceived as being more elitist than those from Burundi, who have a higher status than returnees from the DRC. Tutsi who stayed in Rwanda and survived the genocide are suspected of collaboration with the *génocidaires*, for it is doubted that any Tutsi could have survived on their own. There are also divisions between Hutu who participated in the killings, those who are suspected of being involved, and those who did not participate. The genocide, while reinforcing the split between Hutu and Tutsi, also created new social cleavages that run within ethnic groups. Cross-cutting social capital should be nurtured to link not only Hutu and Tutsi but also those within the subgroups. Overcoming the new schisms and reconciling old differences may take generations.

Violent conflict and the political and economic disintegration of the Rwandan state destroyed whatever broad-based forms of social capital had existed. The conflict deeply penetrated such forms of horizontal social capital as exchange, mutual assistance, collective action, trust, and protection of the vulnerable. During the conflict, vertical relations were reinforced; in the postconflict years, these relations have suffered (see Table 4). Thus, postconflict social capital, although somewhat mirroring preconflict conditions, has undergone change in different ways.

The use of credit in exchanges was common in preconflict Rwanda. This practice has diminished over time, in part due to decreased levels of trust as a consequence of warfare but also because of increasing poverty and the value placed on money and individualism. In general, those interviewed felt that people have become more reluctant to give gifts and provide for the needs of others, for they are less confident that these acts will be reciprocated.

Environmental degradation, isolation, and scarcity have also caused exchange to dwindle. Diminishing soil fertility and scarcity of land and water in Giti have hurt the productivity of both agriculture and cattle herding. These conditions have led to a decrease in secondary or associational social capital by diminishing the ability to exchange goods and services. During the genocide, Giti isolated itself from neighboring communes out of fear. It has remained somewhat distant, with limited external market penetration, which has hampered economic activity. As a result, poverty within Giti is increasing, causing even further reductions in exchange, mutual assistance, and gift giving.

Extreme and widespread poverty in Shyanda, along with a decline in the availability of goods and labor, has hampered economic activity, primarily because of loss of or damage to resources and the weakening of social capital as a result of the conflict. Agriculture is now almost the sole economic activity, but the

Table 4   Interactions between violent conflict and social capital: Rwanda

	High-conflict period	Low-conflict period
High social capital	Protection across ethnic lines: some Hutu helped protect Tutsi during the war, as was the case in Giti (and some Tutsi risked their lives to save others). Within the Interahamwe and between extremist Hutu, bonding social capital united groups by manipulating and employing excellent information networks, collective action, civic duty, solidarity, mutual benefit, common goals and shared activity, and traditions.	Family relations (nuclear and extended); intermarriage between Hutu and Tutsi. Multiethnic associations: Old: agriculture, cattle herding (beneficial to commune) New: widows' and orphans' groups (exclusive, beneficial to members only). *Gacaca* (a traditional mechanism for dispute mediation and distributive justice) in the pre- and postconflict eras. Mutual assistance; gift giving; sharing of beer, necessities, and crops resurfaced but were not as prevalent. Cooperation on communal buildings and projects such as road maintenance.
Low social capital	Killing within communities and families. Cessation by associations and community groups of communal activities such as farming and events such as meetings and markets. Cessation of almost all government activities; no services were provided during the war. Because of the government's involvement in the killings, moderate Hutu and Tutsi had little trust in the government. Strong vertical social capital superseded horizontal relations and alliances.	Divisions within families, not just between communities (postconflict). Decreased sense of trust and candor between individuals (postconflict). Perceived decrease in social capital due to modernization, individualism, and monetization. Local-to-global shift and move from primary bonds to secondary linkages perceived as decrease in social capital. Perception that traditions began to diminish with colonization and the influx of Catholicism.

ravages of war have decreased crop productivity and made fewer people available to work in the fields. There are also fewer men to contribute to the financial and physical needs of the community, as many have been killed or are currently in prison. As a result, the burden on women and children has increased tremendously.

This increased burden has not been offset by cooperation and mutual assistance, both of which have decreased in the communes. Giti, although not directly affected by the fighting, experienced much damage during the war. Large numbers of displaced persons sought refuge in the commune, destroying and damaging buildings and straining resources. Now, high levels of poverty have made commune members less able to provide for the needs of others, and increasing monetization within the society has made them less likely to give gifts and assistance.

The existence and nature of associations and the reason for their creation (whether based on shared interests or on prescribed commonality, as in familial relations) were dramatically affected by the genocide and the perversion of social bonds. During the conflict, especially in 1994, farming activity stopped across the country (except, perhaps, for small efforts by individual families), and the cooperative associations that oversaw these activities disbanded. Since the war, the associations and other informal networks have revived out of necessity. These organizations, which primarily deal with the legacies of the war, are geared toward vulnerable groups and help meet their own members' basic survival needs. Whereas prewar associations strove to better the welfare of people internal and external to the group, the new organizations are predominantly exclusive, although some include both Tutsi and Hutu. For example, widows' and orphans' associations have emerged in both communes to assist each of these vulnerable groups. In Giti, orphans' associations have arisen to provide funds for schooling. In Shyanda, despite the genocidal experience there, both Hutu and Tutsi cooperate in widows' and orphans' associations. Still, there is an underlying feeling of mistrust and resentment. In one widows' association that includes both Hutu women whose husbands are in prison and Tutsi women whose husbands were killed during the war, members who were interviewed stated that they work together, but only for their survival. They do not feel that they can deal or speak with each other openly. This guarded or limited cross-cutting social capital has emerged out of shared circumstances, isolation, and new social cleavages, not trust.

Many of those interviewed felt that the dissolution of families, which has occurred in both communes, has led to the creation of the new types of association. To some extent, people have turned to associations to make up for their lack of family ties, which were at times strengthened during the conflict but, overall, were greatly harmed as a result of the extremes to which violence was carried. Respondents also noted that relations between families joined through marriage have been greatly weakened: in-laws can no longer rely on each other for support and assistance. Even the nuclear family has failed to a degree. Fathers and brothers are dead or in jail, and mothers, struggling to fill the role of the missing men, often cannot meet the needs of their children. Some children are sent away from home to live with extended family or to wander the streets in hopes that aid or religious organizations will be able to assist them.

According to respondents, intermarriage still occurs between Hutu and Tutsi in Giti and Shyanda, but it is often criticized in the wake of the genocide. Commune members in Giti are reluctant to marry those outside their own commune for fear of marrying into a murderous family.

Thus, most dimensions of horizontal social capital were negatively affected by the war, yet in the postwar period they are being revived in various forms to help restore some sense of normalcy. Exchange within and between groups is occurring again but at a lower level and in altered forms, as a result of the conflict and its legacy, as well as modernizing factors. Feelings of solidarity, as evidenced by acts of mutual assistance and collective action, have also dwindled; when they do persist, their motivations have changed. Vulnerable groups are protected, but more by self-help than through a community effort to support them. And trust, a key element in social capital, is still lacking to a large extent in both communes or, if present, is fragile.

Vertical Influences and External Factors

Vertical relations in Rwanda have traditionally had a great influence over society. Tutsi kings were considered almost divine and were revered and followed faithfully. With independence in the early 1960s, this vertical control continued as Hutu power was consolidated in a strong central government. Traditional and informal local leadership dissipated and was replaced by administrators appointed by the national government.

Strong vertical influence may have helped spare Giti during the genocide, thanks to the actions of its burgomaster, or communal head, who forbade killing in his commune. Giti was also an early point of entry for the RPF. Conversely, in Shyanda, which initially escaped violence and in fact served as a Tutsi refuge, killings began soon after orders were dispatched by the acting prime minister, a Hutu from the region, who visited the commune to reproach it for its failure to mount a genocidal response. In this case, strong vertical alliances overpowered horizontal allegiance, with tragic results (Des Forges 1999). Since the war, the official communal leadership has maintained high levels of control over the communes. Local leadership remains under central control, although the national government is making strong efforts to decentralize.

According to many of those interviewed, social capital has also been transformed by factors external to warfare—mainly those related to modernization: market penetration, monetization, and individualism—and, more indirectly, changes stemming from colonialism and the historical influence of the Catholic Church. Study participants felt that there had been a decrease in the level and a change in the nature of both primary bonding relations and secondary bridging linkages in both communes. The majority of those interviewed viewed "traditional" social capital as localized, primary relations among extended family and small communities that provided welfare mechanisms and social protection. Participants in the study felt that moves toward developmental and economic linkages with those outside the community had weakened primary social capital. Interestingly, participants did not consider the strengthening of inter-communal relations and trade and the rise of new forms of associations as the continuation of social capital, albeit transformed; rather, they viewed these changes as an erosion of the Rwandan social fabric. According to those interviewed, increasing monetization and individualism, as well as widespread and worsening poverty, were to blame for the decrease in mutual assistance and gift giving within communes. Overall, external factors to the conflict, and the conflict itself, were considered reasons for the many transformations of social capital in Rwanda since the prewar period.

The shaping of social capital in Rwanda is clearly at a crossroads. The challenge is to balance economic development with social development in a manner that enables the nation to find its way out of the darkness of poverty while both encouraging social relations that cross class, ethnic, and gender divides and preserving the primary ties that serve as the bedrock of societal life. Inclusive state institutions and conflict-management mechanisms need to be encouraged and supported for a cohesive society to thrive. Many positive signs of steps in this direction have already emerged, such as the bridging widows' and orphans' associations; government moves toward decentralization and increasing participation; the revival of *gacaca*; and a more accountable civil administration.

4

Guatemala and Somalia: Violent Conflict and the State

The nature and duration of conflict in Guatemala and Somalia provide differing contexts for the analysis of the interrelations of social capital and conflict in each country. The war in Guatemala spanned almost four decades. There, an absolute, oppressive state targeted indigenous groups and peasants and polarized relations between the state and the predominantly Mayan peasantry. In Somalia, by contrast, the turmoil mounted over the span of a decade. Failed state policies that bloated the military and the civil service and coerced divisiveness among Somalis sped the government's dissolution and the consequent eruption of clan warfare. These differing situations led to consistent or similar findings, especially regarding the ways in which state and market forces interact with violent conflict and social capital to shape social cohesion or disintegration.

Study Methodology

The studies in Guatemala and Somalia were conducted by CERFE, an Italian research NGO that has had prolonged field experience in both countries. Research began with a literature review that analyzed materials on the countries' histories and on work related to social capital. During this phase, surveys to be used in the field were drafted and were translated into Spanish and Somali. Field research, which was conducted between July 1998

51

and February 1999, was led by CERFE staff and was implemented by a local field manager and indigenous interviewers. Each in-country group received extensive training on the tools to be utilized and on survey implementation. Pretests were used to refine the survey before its implementation.

As in the Cambodia and Rwanda studies, two towns were chosen in each country, one less affected by conflict and the other marked by intense conflict. In Somalia the town of Hargeisa experienced more trauma and violence than its counterpart, Boroma. (Both are in Somaliland in the northwest, an area that has a functioning government, state institutions, and civil society associations such as councils of elders, NGOs, and religious organizations that bridge social divisions.) In Guatemala the town of Nebaj experienced more conflict than did Puerto Barrios. Although efforts were made to select matched pairs, controlling for the level of violence, there were difficulties in demographically pairing the towns. Consequently, there are discrepancies in size, ethnic composition, and socioeconomic levels. Hargeisa has a population of 295,000, with 141 identified civil society groups, and Boroma has a population of 64,000, with 63 identified civil society groups. Puerto Barrios has a population of 82,000 (170 identified civil society groups); Nebaj has a population of 55,000 (187 identified civil society groups).

In contrast to the studies in Cambodia and Rwanda, which distinctly endeavored to assess pre- and postconflict social capital, CERFE focused more on making a detailed sketch of the present postconflict civil society within each country and on measuring its ability to provide services and economic opportunity for its communities, especially with regard to vertically penetrating state and market engagement. This orientation meshes nicely with the failed-state syndrome frequently ascribed to Somalia and the oppressive-state framework applied to Guatemala (Zartman and Kremenyuk 1995).

The first phase of the field research sought to identify the socially responsible collective actors that together made up civil society by contributing to the well-being of the community. Eighty-five organizations were surveyed in Hargeisa, 44 in Boroma, 51 in Nebaj, and 50 in Puerto Barrios. Interviews were conducted with key informants, leaders at the local level, and civil servants. In the second phase, CERFE studied the quality of leadership in a selected number of these groups. A total of 84 leaders in both countries was interviewed. In the final phase, organizations were studied in depth—20 in Guatemala and 21 in Somalia—and their leaders (totaling 41) were interviewed. Also questioned in the final phase were 52 key informants and 94 citizens who were not members of the organizations being studied. (Copies of the survey instruments are available from the authors on request.)

Social Responsibility, Social Initiative, and Violent Conflict

CERFE established a single framework and methodology for examining social capital in Guatemala and Somalia.[7] The concept of social capital was restricted to civic engagement in the protection and development of communities, encompassing social capital at the communal level that includes both the protective functions of primary-group relations and the development aspects of secondary cross-cutting relations. The model does not assess primary or bonding levels of social capital, such as kin-based and tightly knit communal relationships, per se. Instead, it focuses on civil society's protective provision of basic survival needs and its ability to create fertile ground for economic growth and development.

According to CERFE's approach, *social capital* is the presence of two autonomous dimensions of civil society: social responsibility and social initiative. *Civil society* is defined as a set of collective actors geared toward social action that includes (but is not considered exclusive to) actors from schools, churches, the media, the private sector, NGOs, and universities. Such social action is either "welfare" or "development" oriented.

Social responsibility is seen as civil society's capacity to act as a self-defense mechanism for the community at large, providing people with social protection or welfare when society is threatened by such risks as health crises, illiteracy, unemployment, lack of access to higher education, geographic isolation, and conflict. This ability is considered to be affected by the degree of diversification within civil society and the number and quality of civil society actors.

Social initiative is viewed as civil society's engagement in efforts toward economic growth and development. This potential differs according to the diversification and quality of actors, local factors, and normative obstacles. Local factors consist of confidence and trust, material opportunities (communications, mobility, infrastructure; and education, banking, and health services) and cognitive capital (qualified personnel with specific skills). Normative obstacles include factors that are formal or legal, substantive, organizational and bureaucratic, social and cultural, or political in nature. Social initiative is defined as a measure of a specific quality of civil society; that is, its orientation toward economic development. In this regard, it is civil society, not other entities, that has greater or lesser social initiative.

Together, levels of social responsibility and social initiative make up the larger construct of social capital. Civil society can tend toward social responsibility that is insular and more protective in nature, as is often the case in conditions of intense violent conflict, when trust is at a premium. Alternatively, it can possess social capital that is more networked, outward-looking, and development oriented or is geared toward social initiative, as may be the case in periods of peace and security. These two aspects of social capital (much like the notions of bonding and bridging social capital) may vary in their interplay with conflict, the quality of civil society, and the penetration and role of the state and market forces. In this way, the study examines civil society as a composite of two types of social capital that may substitute for or complement state and market roles and functions, revealing the degree of social cohesion—the intersection between state- and market-driven vertical or linking social capital and civil society–driven horizontal or bridging social capital.

The *violent conflict indicators* (see Box 4) employed in Guatemala and Somalia were chosen by the researchers to enable comparison of the effects of the conflicts in the two countries. Despite the problems in ascertaining the exact period of conflict, various indicators were established to assess the conflicts, such as acts of

---

Box 4 Indicators of violent conflict: Guatemala and Somalia

- Possession by common citizens of weapons for self-defense
- Shootings over the past 12 months
- Outbreaks of violence caused by the presence of armed troops
- Evacuation of staffs of international bodies over the past 12 months
- Kidnapping of people for noncriminal reasons
- Need for foreigners to use armed escorts
- Raids or pillaging
- Human rights violations
- Violence against, or disappearance or kidnapping of, politicians, unionists, and other public representatives
- Unlawful executions
- Armed outbreaks among representatives of parties and political movements
- Crowd violence or riots
- Police interventions to repress public demonstrations
- High levels of common crime, such as theft, robbery, acts of violence, organized crime, and murder; presence of illicit trading
- Presence of roadblocks controlled by armed soldiers
- Presence of armed troops
- Existence of unsafe areas
- Presence of organizations devoted to self-defense of the population
- Presence of death squads
- Disruption of education and health services delivery
- Destruction of infrastructure and natural resources
- Loss of market and financial resources
- Presence of refugees and displaced populations

---

violence, the presence of armed troops, and damage to infrastructure and market forces.

The periods of conflict selected differed in length. The war in Guatemala lasted 35 years, making it difficult to assess pre-conflict social capital. To take this into consideration, the conflict period was associated with the time of the most intense fighting, 1980–83. The Somali government fell only eight years ago, but conditions had been deteriorating since the end of the Ogaden war with Ethiopia in 1976, and interviewees had difficulty in describing the preconflict period.

Guatemala: The State against the People

The 35 years of civil war in Guatemala resulted in roughly 180,000 killings, 40,000 "disappearances," the destruction of more than 400 villages, internal displacement of over 1 million people, and the flight of 100,000 refugees to neighboring countries. Severe social, economic, and political exclusion was a catalyst for the protracted, brutal conflict, and these exclusionary issues remain only partially resolved after the peace accord. Current tensions, as before, are firmly rooted in the exceedingly inequitable distribution of resources; 70 percent of the arable land belongs to 3 percent of Guatemalans, and roughly 80 percent of the population lives in poverty (Costello 1995).

The civil war began in 1960 with a failed nationalist uprising against corruption by army officers, who then sought refuge in rural areas and formed a guerrilla army. The movement was initially aligned with Cuban revolutionary forces and was consolidated within Ladino (Spanish-speaking) regions.[8] However, "over the next two decades, political and social reforms became a rallying point, with the indigenous populations playing a major role" (Kostner, Nezam, and Scott 1997: 2). Ethnic differences were at the root of the unequal distribution of resources, which was rigidified by the racist, exclusive political structure that promoted Ladino interests and culture. Mayan communities became politicized as a response to these historical injustices and the influence of liberation theology. Many of the guerrilla movements, although led by disenfranchised Ladinos, recruited large numbers of Mayans and were based in indigenous highland areas. By incorporating Mayan concerns into their program for struggle, guerrilla forces augmented their troops and widened the scope of their cause.

Demands for greater freedom and democracy in the mid- to late 1970s were met with new waves of repression, involving massacres, death threats, and the assassination of local leaders and activists. Warfare became even more brutal and vicious and was targeted toward eliminating the Mayan people living in areas where the guerrillas operated. Entire sectors of the population became military targets for the state. In 1981–83 alone, over 100,000 civilians were killed. It was in this period that most of the internal displacement, forcible relocations, and refugee movements caused by the war took place. Concurrently, a highland deforestation campaign was undertaken to remove physical cover for guerrillas. As hostilities mounted, the guerrilla groups and the Communist Guatemalan Workers Party (PGT) aligned in 1982 to form the Guatemalan National Revolutionary Union (URNG). By this time, however, the poorly armed guerrillas were unable to defend their supporters in the rural highlands against the full weight of military violence (Costello 1995).

The large-scale massacres were generally over by 1984. The army set up new bases throughout the Mayan heartland and greatly increased its own wealth by seizing productive land and important state institutions. It consolidated control over rural populations by setting up model government villages that received returning refugees and displaced people. The army also organized an intense militarization campaign, recruiting civilian males over the age of 16 into civil defense patrols (PACs). Although recruitment was supposedly voluntary, those who refused were considered guerrilla sympathizers. The PACs guarded towns, verified villagers' identification, reported any suspicious activities, and assisted in searches for guerrilla movements; they consequently increased the divisions and suspicions within indigenous communities. The PACs reached their height in the mid-1980s, when they had about 900,000 members (Costello 1995).

Throughout the early 1980s, the government's counter-insurgency campaigns exacerbated the original causes of the conflict. Displacement and resettlement worsened already grave land scarcity and distribution problems. In addition, the political structure was far from democratic, for army and military commissioners were the only state representatives in the highlands. City authorities were obliged to require prior approval for gatherings of more than two people. Centralization of power continued to increase, and there was a total absence of accountability.

Indigenous groups and those in rural areas bore the brunt of these mounting injustices.

A transition toward peace began around the mid-1980s with the adoption of a new constitution, the election of a civilian president, and the introduction of political pluralism and personal liberties. Concurrently, preparations were made for negotiations, involving consultations with political parties, the private sector, religious groups, academics, labor unions, and other members of civil society. Formal discussions between the URNG and the newly formed government commission for peace (COPAZ) began in 1991, and in 1994 civil society was brought into the negotiations. The final peace agreement, signed in December 1996, brought together accords on democratization, human rights, displaced populations, indigenous rights, socioeconomic issues, and the role of civil society and the military.

Somalia: State Disintegration, Anarchy, and Resilience

In Guatemala state warfare against the people resulted in the centralization of government power and reactionary policies of violence and fear as a means of maintaining control; in Somalia it led to the disintegration of the state.

From the time it overthrew Somalia's civilian government in 1969, the military government of General Siad Barre engaged in systematic repression and elimination of civil society actors in an attempt to maintain absolute control For the first decade, this was done through the ideology of "scientific socialism," which called for the suppression of private initiative, the undermining of any form of civil action not sanctioned by the state, and the dismantling of centers of traditional authority (bonding social capital). The public execution of religious leaders for disagreeing with Barre on the interpretation of the Quran was a major turning point in community-government relations in this highly religious society, greatly deepening public fear and distrust of the government. The alienation of society was further entrenched by the widespread arrests of Western-trained intellectuals, the imprisonment of those suspected of disloyalty, the establishment of "orientation centers" for the indoctrination of the population, and the holding of mass rallies to propagate the "revolutionary ideology." These government efforts sought to reengineer the society and cultivate a personality cult along the lines of certain communist regimes. This further eroded the traditional values that provided the foundations for social cohesion. A ubiquitous security apparatus created fear and suspicion among individuals and groups. The firing of civil servants (often the most competent ones) suspected of less than total loyalty to the "revolution" severely undermined state institutional capacity and integrity. These measures had the effect of highly centralizing authority, degrading state institutions, and undermining civil society and informal social relations.

After the U.S.S.R. backed Ethiopia in the 1977–78 Ogaden war between Somalia and Ethiopia, the Barre government switched alliances from the Eastern socialist bloc to the West. To maintain power, the regime abandoned socialist rhetoric and solicited and obtained the support of the United States. Concurrently, it sought the support of some clans and targeted certain other clans for collective punishment, striking out against the Majerteen clan of the northeast (some of whose members were implicated in a military coup in 1978). A scorched-earth campaign targeting both people and their means of their livelihood was begun in this area. The absence of any meaningful reaction by other Somalis to the plight of their brethren reflected both the pervasive fear of the government and an unraveling of cross-cutting social ties and traditional values. The government's actions demonstrated that any form of organized opposition would be met with maximum force, and many people remained docile. In 1988 a full-scale military assault was launched against the Issak clan in northern Somalia (present Somaliland), destroying all the major urban centers and scattering most of the urban population into Ethiopia as refugees. The army systematically destroyed or looted all valuable assets in most urban centers and spread anti-personnel mines to prevent the return of refugees.

Despite its efforts to maintain power, the Barre government, with its legitimacy forfeited and the army disintegrating, collapsed in 1991. Its dissolution unleashed the legacies of decades of repression: "a culture of vengeance," a ready supply of weapons acquired through Cold War politics, intense interclan hatreds, and a failed economy in which clans fought over what few resources were left (Menkhaus 1998: 220–21). By the time Barre fled the capital in January 1991, some members of the armed forces were already engaged in looting embassies and public property. Warlords drew on bonding social capital to create private armies, mainly made up of fellow clan members, that dominated groups with no access to weapons. (The shared experience in turn reinforced the bonds within the armed groups.) Violent conflict erupted across Somalia over control of economic resources and visible assets: the port and airport of the capital, Mogadishu; rich agricultural lands; and the southern port city of Kismayo.

The sudden collapse of an internationally recognized state without any external force or threat was a unique event in the history of nations. The self-inflicted implosion brought misery to millions of Somalis, setting off a prolonged famine and mass starvation and ushering in a decade of anarchy and violence. These events not only destroyed the asset base of the country and the accumulated gains of generations; they claimed hundreds of thousands of lives and led to the displacement of thousands of Somalis within and outside the country's boundaries.

State-sponsored violence and the systematic destruction of social capital during Barre's military dictatorship not only planted the seeds of the disintegration of the state but also nurtured intergroup enmities. No societal glue was left to hold the nation together once the formal state structures collapsed. The disintegration of the state resulted in a different kind of violence—decentralized, clan-based, and driven by the desire to settle old scores or the struggle over resources. Violence was often either anarchic or led by warlords who had been able to appropriate significant caches of weaponry.

The earlier experience during the military campaign against Hargeisa and other cities, when many members of the armed forces engaged in looting at considerable gain and without being held accountable, may have demonstrated the potential benefits and low risks of looting. The interclan conflicts that followed were mainly over control of resources. Warlords recruited uneducated, armed young men to fuel their "economies of plunder" (Menkhaus 1998: 221). These renegade groups, whose new status and wealth would evaporate if peace and stability were restored, have worked to undermine UN and other peace efforts (Adam and Ford 1998).

External peace efforts repeatedly failed due to a lack of understanding of the situation. Negotiations involved members of the 16 recognized factions battling throughout Somalia, but external actors failed to realize that these factions lacked the legitimacy to rule even over the territory they claimed. The ability to govern had devolved to a much more local level. The UN mission left Somalia in 1995 without successfully establishing a national government. Anarchy, however, did not ensue. Since then, violent conflict has plagued parts of southern Somalia, but it has remained localized.

Although efforts to set up a centralized government failed, some areas—notably, the self-proclaimed Somaliland Republic (the former British Somaliland) in the northwest and Puntland in the northeast—have reestablished markets, services and service delivery, and minimal forms of governance. (Box 5 describes a successful grassroots initiative to create local government structures.) This progress had been driven by traditional Somali authorities such as elders and religious leaders, businessmen, and women's associations (Menkhaus 1998). Relative peace and security and a high degree of social responsibility and civic action, including a vibrant private sector, continue to prevail in those two areas. Coincidentally, these areas had also been the targets of widespread government atrocities against the civilian population. The shared experience of victimization may have contributed to a buildup of bonding social capital in these two areas.

The emergence of market forces, even in areas where open conflict continues, often tends to mitigate conflict and raise the cost of looting; owners of private property are likely to seek redress, with the support of relatives and clan members, and to pursue perpetrators. Exchange of goods and services between clans and areas encourages cross-cutting ties and creates a vested interest in minimizing open conflict. Markets have also been able

---

Box 5   The Boroma Conference: a bottom-up approach to reconciliation

In recent years, a number of reconciliation conferences and other initiatives aiming at bringing together the warring factions in Somalia have been sponsored by various parties, including the UN, the Organization of African Unity (OAU), the Arab League, and neighboring countries—but none succeeded. Substantial amounts of donor money were spent in organizing these conferences. The participants were mainly the various faction leaders, many of them responsible for past or ongoing tragedies, and the meetings were often held in overseas locations. There was usually no community or grassroots participation in the selection of participants or even in setting the agenda. The conferences were mainly top-to-bottom initiatives, with the factions usually posturing for external audiences rather than talking to each other.

A contrasting case was a conference held in Boroma, Somaliland, in 1995 attended by about 2,000 delegates representing practically all the main communities, clans, and localities. The conference, patterned after traditional peace meetings, lasted for more than three months, without a time limit. It was locally organized and financed, and it addressed grievances and differences at the local level before moving to formal governance issues, state structures, and power-sharing arrangements. At the end of the conference, a president and a parliament were elected, and various interclan conflicts were settled. The Boroma conference succeeded where larger, externally driven, top-down conferences did not.

---

to provide essential goods and services, sometimes more effectively than when there was an internationally recognized government. The absence of restrictive government policies has tended to encourage competition and entrepreneurship.

Infrastructure services—such as telecommunications, power, and transportation, including air—which had been provided by the public sector are now provided by the local private sector. Efficient trading systems have enabled Somali traders to penetrate markets in neighboring countries and remain competitive. The private sector, which is seldom bound by regional and tribal or clan divisions, acts as an integrating factor. The livestock trade (the linchpin of the Somali economy), money transfer, transportation, and telecommunications are all interregional and therefore highly integrative. Private activity has been most active in areas where relative security prevails. Thus there is a relatively vibrant private sector around the northeast port of Bosaso (in Puntland) and in Somaliland. In Hargeisa, Somaliland, for example, there are four competing telephone service providers with rates that are internationally competitive. There is a relative boom in real estate and construction, and efficient trade and banking services. A local private airline (Dallo Airlines) links Hargeisa not only with other cities of Somalia but also with several international destinations: Jeddah, Dubai, Addis Ababa, and Djibouti. A money transfer company (Dahabshil), started by a local entrepreneur, has branches in many parts of the world and connects Somalis in the diaspora with relatives at home. It can transfer money from most major cites in Europe, North America, and the Middle East to relatives anywhere in Somalia, or between different localities inside Somalia, within a couple of days.

Civil society, including religious organizations, and clan elders have played a significant role in mediating interclan conflicts and encouraging cross-cutting activities. Religious groups, which are active even where hostilities have not yet ceased, have provided health and education services and have in some instances supplied food to orphans and poor families. These groups often transcend clan and regional lines, thus helping strengthen cross-cutting social capital. The role of civil society in containing conflict is most evident in Somaliland, where traditional leadership and authority have remained relatively intact, despite the efforts of the last central government to subvert it. Clan leaders are often most effective in building bonding capital between members of a group and mediating conflict within that group, but they have also been successful in mediating and containing conflict between groups and clans in areas of relative calm. These traditional leaders have been the main element in restraining interclan conflict and in laying the basis for the emergence of civil authority. They are least effective in areas where there is still open conflict or that are run by warlords.

The Impact of State and Market Forces on Social Cohesion in Guatemala and Somalia

The Somali and Guatemalan governments both struck out against their peoples in their attempts to maintain control over power and resources. Indigenous and rural groups in Guatemala fought to gain political, economic, and social rights and, in particular, access to land. Campaigns by the government to eradicate the "enemy" led to years of violence across the Guatemalan countryside. Social initiative moves by civil society finally ushered in peace after almost four decades of warfare and extermination.

The Somali government tried to suppress all forms of opposition and in the process fell into anarchy, with clan battling clan over power. To counter this chaos, socially responsible religious groups have provided education and health services. Although hostilities have not ceased in Somalia, various types of social initiative have emerged. Many women's groups have tried to promote peacemaking, and globalization, especially in the form of market penetration, has facilitated successful moves toward stability in the northwestern and northeastern regions.

According to conventional wisdom, the higher the capacity of civil society for social responsibility and social initiative, the higher the level of social capital. The study results show how the effect of conflict on the two dimensions of social capital differed in the countries studied (see Tables 5 and 6).

The study results reveal the relationship between the development of civil society and violent conflict is not totally predictable. War causes the decay and, in severe situations, the weakening of civil society, particularly by reinforcing bonding, inward-looking social capital in the quest for survival often inadvertently undermining cross-cutting social capital that may bridge diverse communal groups. Yet, as this study indicates, in some situations civil society may continue to be active, or may thrive even as fighting continues, by providing welfare and protection services in volatile regions—thus supplanting primary relations, and in more secure areas, creating the space and connectivity that market forces require.

Table 5   Interactions between violent conflict and social capital: Guatemala

	High-conflict period	Low-conflict period
High social capital	Emergence of groups that provided social welfare and protective mechanisms during and immediately after conflict, such as the numerous NGOs and other civil society groups. Religious leaders who led liberation theology movements and who, with their followers, were often targeted by the state for their beliefs and actions. Organizations of Guatemalan women who united to promote peacemaking Traditional Mayan institutions, such as Maya spirituality, that provided a safety net for communities affected by violence, and national Maya organizations that united to fight for the recognition of their rights during the peace negotiations and in the reconstruction process.	Traditional Guatemalan structures, such as the *alcaldes auxiliares*, who were elected by their communities and were charged with representing them in the municipal government. They had some administrative, judiciary, and police functions and were charged with local dispute resolution.
Low social capital	Targeting of the state's own constituents during the war. This was a central policy of the military authorities and was facilitated by the breakdown of the legal system and democratic controls, which then allowed the violation of human rights. Human rights violations often took the form of private violence implemented by secret and paramilitary organizations on orders from high political figures. In most cases, the violence took place away from the theater of war, often striking people not directly involved in either political affairs or guerrilla warfare. The system implemented to perpetrate these crimes was deeply rooted in the country. This military policy further eroded relations between the people and the government.	Discrimination against the Mayas, which has been, and remains, imbedded in Guatemalan culture, preventing the creation of cross-cutting social capital. Lack of cross-cutting social capital, evidenced by the historically poor relations be-

(Table continues on next page.)

Table 5 *(continued)*

High-conflict period	*Low-conflict period*
Schisms within communities as some villagers joined government-supported civil defense patrols (PACs). The PACs, along with military commissars, replaced the traditional *alcaldes auxiliares*.	tween indigenous groups and the Ladinos. Although social capital within each group may have been high or stable, the lack of bridging social capital has prevented understanding between them.
Adverse effects on other social structures and traditional figures. Elders, whose authority had already been weakened by Catholic catechists, were further undermined by repression. *Cofradías*, traditional religious structures, lost their ability to carry on their complex rituals during the war, and their leaders (*mayordomos*) lost much of their authority.	

Table 6   Interactions between violent conflict and social capital: Somalia

	High-conflict period	Low-conflict period
High social capital	Emergence of a de facto government in Hargeisa able to provide services and order. Increased market penetration through the diaspora, promoting cross-cutting ties. Emergence of women's initiatives during the conflict, uniting clans through trade and economic activities ("Green-Line markets"). Provision by religious institutions of services such as education and health care that the government was unable to provide.	Somali elders from different clans managed and resolved conflict by using as guidance customary laws that regulated and curbed potential conflict within or between clans. Elders thus retained a critical function in Somali society through their important role in negotiations with other groups and as mediators for their own communities. In theory, elders did not have authoritative power to determine the outcome of a conflict; rather, they represented the preferences of their clans. Alliance of clans through marriage, which established social and economic ties between the groups.
Low social capital	Dissolution of the state government of Somalia. Clashes between clans vying for control of power, territory, and resources. Inability of clans to successfully negotiate a peace agreement despite numerous international, regional, and local efforts.	The chronic disconnect between the Somali state and its people. Lack of government organizational integrity and synergistic relations throughout the country's independence, except for a short period of a few years.

Social responsibility and the level of violent conflict did seem to be positively correlated. Study results revealed that the social responsibility of civil society seemed to be more active in both Nebaj and Hargeisa than in communities not as traumatized by war. This development, which was attributed to the need to secure basic needs and ensure survival, emerged in both conflict areas during or soon after the conflict. Thus, war would seem to have a positive impact on mobilizing families and tightly knit communities to become socially responsible in ensuring communal protection and survival, predominantly welfare functions.

The results of the study failed to explain unambiguously how conflict affected social initiative—that is, civil society's ability to nurture economic growth and development. In general, levels of social initiative were affected less by conflict than by other factors, primarily confidence, material opportunities, cognitive capital, and normative obstacles. (It should, however, be noted that conflict does directly affect these factors and thus indirectly influences social initiative.) Puerto Barrios and Hargeisa had relatively high social initiative levels despite mixed experiences with conflict. (Puerto Barrios was less traumatized than Nebaj, while Hargeisa was exposed to more conflict than Boroma.) A reason for this mixed result may be that Puerto Barrios and Hargeisa are larger than their counterparts and, perhaps because of their size, have higher levels of market penetration. Puerto Barrios suffered less damage to its infrastructure (roads and communications) than did Nebaj, while Hargeisa's infrastructure benefited from an engaged and active diaspora committed to reinvesting in and rebuilding northern Somalia. These outside contacts, in combination with weak state penetration and, therefore, fewer financial regulations, expedited growth in Hargeisa. This, in turn, provided an opening for the formation of bridging social capital through the marketplace.

Overall, the study findings appear to illustrate interesting facets of the two dimensions of social capital—social responsibility and social initiative, or horizontal social capital—in response to varying levels of state and market penetration (vertical social capital). Of the two hard-hit towns, Nebaj had a high social responsibility level and a low social initiative level, whereas

Hargeisa had high levels of social responsibility and social initiative. Puerto Barrios had lower levels of social responsibility and higher levels of social initiative, and Boroma exhibited lower levels of both social responsibility and social initiative.

The findings in Guatemala stem from varying degrees of state penetration and demographics. Nebaj was one of the main areas where the army fully prosecuted its counterinsurgency strategy, with PACs being established in all communities. The town, which is roughly 95 percent Maya-Ixil, turned inward in response to the discriminatory and violent practices of the state. Puerto Barrios was less touched by violence, had a more mixed Ladino and Mayan population (with some blacks and Garifunas, or black Caribs), and was less affected by state penetration through the counterinsurgency efforts than its counterpart Nebaj. It scored high on social initiative but low on social responsibility. This translates into specific types of horizontal and vertical social capital that differed between the towns, with Nebaj exemplifying primary bonding social capital and Puerto Barrios tilting toward bridging social capital.

In short, where there was space, civil society in Guatemala reacted by forming bridging social capital. Where there was discrimination and oppression, civil society contracted into insular, bonding social capital. In some cases, traditional Mayan institutions, such as Mayan spirituality and community structures, provided a safety net for those most affected by violence, while national Mayan organizations united to fight for the recognition of their rights during the peace negotiations and in the reconstruction process.

Thus, although there may be some interaction between social responsibility and social initiative, they appear to diverge during heightened periods of conflict, with a kind of survivalist retreat into primary bonding social capital taking place especially among the discriminated-against Mayan population. This is not unlike the behavior of Cambodians, and the Tutsi of Rwanda during the height of organized state violence in those societies.

In examining civil society's capacity for social responsibility and social initiative in Guatemala and Somalia, the role of the state and market forces is evident. Mapping the functions and responsibilities of civil society revealed the inadequacies and the strengths of the state and the involvement of the external market. Civil society in both countries substituted for state roles by becoming the main provider of safety nets and basic services, especially for vulnerable groups in the context of a failed state (in Somalia) and an oppressive, exclusionary state (in Guatemala). In Somalia, and to a lesser extent in Guatemala, the effects of globalization, in the form of external vertical market penetration and the spread of technology, facilitated the formation of bridging horizontal social capital and the establishment of relative peace and development by making possible social space, exchange, and economic growth.

On the basis of these initial findings, a closer examination of social capital as the ability of civil society to engage in social responsibility and social initiative, and the interrelations of these dimensions with state and market penetration, is needed to shed light on the complex process of indigenous survival, reconstruction, development, and, ultimately, reconciliation in the aftermath of varying degrees of violent conflict.

5

Civic, Market, and State Engagement: A Comparative Analysis

Civic, market, and state engagement under conditions of violent conflict have varying effects on overall social capital formation and societal cohesion. As was true in Cambodia and Rwanda, the degree to which the overall social cohesion of Guatemala and Somalia is realized will be a function of the integration of horizontal social capital—in the form of a thriving civil society (bridging) and strong primary relations (bonding)—with vertical social capital, manifested in dynamic, inclusive state and market engagement. This nexus, in turn, manifests itself in a myriad of cross-cutting social and institutional relations that can serve a conflict management, mediation, and mitigation (prevention) function, the basis for lasting peace and sustainable development. In each of the four case studies, civic engagement emerged both during and immediately after the conflict in the form of mobilization of social protection or activities for growth and development. Market activities emerged in the more stable regions of countries plagued by conflict or in the immediate aftermath period and enabled bridging, intercommunity relations. The interface of the state with social capital and conflict is complex; both the overpowering presence of the state (in Cambodia, Rwanda, and Guatemala) and its absence (in Somalia) led to the disruption of most social relations.

Coping with Violent Conflict: The Role of Civil Society during Warfare

Manifestations of social capital emerged during conflict or immediately after the cessation of hostilities in the form of local, internal coping mechanisms that provided welfare and social protection in each country studied (see Box 6). In this regard, conflict seemingly spurred integrative social capital geared toward mitigating risks within the community. Interestingly, this occurred not only within nuclear and extended families but also within the broader community, encompassing civil society actors. This social capital based on primary associations resembled what had existed in the preconflict period, with slight variations on the previous forms.

Both bonding and bridging social capital emerged within civil society in the form of moves toward welfare and social protection and, to some extent, growth and development (such as efforts to expedite the peace process). During the Heng Samrin period in Cambodia, as the conflict began to wane, traditional types of social capital (for example, pagoda and funeral associations) revived, in forms similar to those before the conflict. In Rwanda, new associations of widows and orphans emerged to provide mutual assistance shortly after the genocide ceased, taking up the traditional roles of families in caring for these vulnerable groups. In Guatemala, Mayan women's associations emerged during the war and served as a catalyst for the peace process, while indigenous groups united through the recreation of institutions for self-protection and promotion, such as the Comunidades de Población en Resistencia (CPR). And in the midst of national conflict, religious institutions in Somalia have established schools and provided health services.

Civic reactions to conflict and its legacies—coping mechanisms—varied by country and type of warfare. In general, coping mechanisms can be internal or external and traditionally range from horizontal social capital relations, such as family, extended family, or clans, to more bridging formal and sometimes vertical organizations such as religious groups, local governments, and markets.

Box 6   Civil society and violent conflict

Cambodia
In traditional Cambodian society, groups that linked non-kin were few. In both villages examined for the study—low-conflict Prasath and high-conflict Prey Koh—some forms of civil society actors existed before the war, but during the conflict, all types of civil society actors ceased to exist. After the cessation of hostilities, civil society actors, notably NGOs involved in socioeconomic development, increased in number and function.

Rwanda
Many efforts were made to strengthen civil society in Rwanda in the late 1980s and early 1990s, in the study villages of Shyanda and Giti as in other places. Yet the existence of civil society actors before the conflict—including cooperatives, credit groups, church-related organizations, and NGOs—did not lead to the growth of cross-cutting social capital, as evidenced by the rapid explosion of the genocide. Civil relations between Hutu and Tutsi quickly evaporated once the state ordered Tutsi elimination. A primary reason was the narrow service orientation of the groups, which were mainly apolitical. Democracy, inclusion, and tolerance did not automatically result from the groups' mere existence; these qualities need to be actively fostered. In the post-genocide setting, new civil society actors are exclusive in that they benefit only their members, but they have served to empower the vulnerable (mainly women and orphans).

Guatemala
During the war, Guatemalan women's organizations were a valuable catalyst for the peace process. Tired of warfare and the resulting destitution and tragedy, these groups began to lobby for a peaceful solution by uniting and involving relevant actors. The conflict has also spurred the growth of numerous associations of indigenous people to protect their existence, way of life, and interests. This has occurred throughout Guatemala, including both study sites, Nebaj and Puerto Barrios. The purposes of the groups range from pursuing political activities to promoting economic initiatives to spur income generation in these mostly impoverished rural regions.

Somalia
In both study sites, Hargeisa and Boroma, religious institutions have arisen to make up for the dearth of state health and education services. Many women's groups have stepped to the forefront of the peace effort, linking warring clans through exchange and women's peace discussions. Civil society in northern Somalia has flourished as a result of the demand for services and market opportunities in the absence of state provision, regulation, and control.

Internal mechanisms include social units, local religious institutions, local political organizations, and economic systems.

- The *social unit,* which includes nuclear and extended families, is the strongest and most basic of all internal coping mechanisms. In crises, families first help themselves, then their relatives, and then their neighbors. During the transition from war to peace, the family is the social unit that is most looked to for emotional recovery.
- *Religious institutions* (churches, mosques, and temples) often provide leadership, comfort, and emotional support in disasters. During reconstruction, they are an excellent entry point for external actors, since they allow direct access to the community through preexisting knowledge, relations, and communications channels.
- *Local political organizations* may provide leadership, supervise external intervention during a crisis, and assist with planning and implementation during reconstruction.
- *Economic coping mechanisms* fall into three types: informal, interpersonal economic relationships; patronage; and mutual assistance organizations such as cooperatives and labor unions. During warfare or crisis, interpersonal economic relationships may emerge as part of the wartime economy, as is the case with much of the entrepreneurship in northern Somalia. Reconstruction efforts can target these informal relations through macro policy and can help spur local growth through microcredit efforts (see Box 7). Mutual assistance organizations such as cooperatives should be sought out as natural counterparts in the delivery of emergency relief and in longer-term reconstruction.

External mechanisms include nonlocal organizations such as NGOs, religious groups, political organizations, economic institutions, social and economic development organizations, and, in some cases, the national government. As Cuny (1994: 84) states in his seminal work, "The effectiveness of external mechanisms depends largely upon their ability to understand and deal with cultural constraints within the host society, their view of development, and their ability to communicate effectively with the

---

Box 7   Women's village banking in Guatemala: building cross-cutting ties through credit

In the highlands of Guatemala, a war-ravaged area, social capital has been restored and is being transformed through village banking. There, the expansion of social networks among rural and semiurban marginalized women is paying financial and social dividends. Often overlooked in studies of microfinance programs is the importance of using social and associational arrangements to promote group solidarity as a means of overcoming the high cost of lending to clients with few assets. Working in high-conflict situations where violence and uncertainty undermine trust and confidence is difficult. Humanitarian assistance programs can compound the problem through paternalistic approaches, turning once self-reliant citizens into passive beneficiaries.

In village banks, trust plays an enormously important role in keeping operations efficient, reducing transaction costs, and smoothing relations. With each successful cycle of lending and repayment, the stock of social capital grows, as trust and confidence are deepened. Staff members of FINCA, the NGO facilitating the Guatemalan banking program, transfers its stock of social capital (networks and relationships), as well as its financial accounting and banking know-how, to Mayan women. The program links the clients to other actors and to private and public information. In effect, it transforms their existing bonding social capital into a broader bridging social capital that, in turn, has spin-off effects on production and marketing and, ultimately, on income and well-being.

Source: Humphreys-Bebbington and Gomez (2000).

---

victims." These groups may become involved during the disaster, in the transition phase, in reconstruction, or in longer-term development. Although this group of external mechanisms does not directly include civil society, it does interface with many civil society actors.

In a crisis, people usually turn to that which is most familiar, and this can enhance coping mechanisms' efficacy and ability to operate. In general, less complex societies, such as rural cultures, have shorter recovery periods. In rural settings, external mechanisms are more effective and efficient if they operate through existing internal mechanisms. Overly intrusive external interventions may inadvertently injure or displace internal coping mechanisms or decrease their effectiveness or their ability to function. In more complex urban settings, it is less likely that internal coping mechanisms will be utilized. External mechanisms then become more appropriate for intervention.

Crises may severely strain indigenous coping mechanisms, whether informal or formal, but they do not destroy them. Often, conflict and disaster act to reinforce these mechanisms and force local organizations to improve their abilities. A major concern is that external interventions may ignore local, spontaneous coping mechanisms, disrupt the internal groups' ability to function, and, in some cases, damage the local coping fabric, undermining the credibility of local efforts within the community. Thus, additive rather than substitutional strategies are the preferred course of action during the transition from emergency to development.

As evidenced in earlier chapters, various forms of survival-based social capital did emerge from within the society during or immediately after the conflict, and these varied according to the nature of conflict that plagued each country. Efforts to reconstruct social capital in the postwar environment must build from these indigenous, spontaneous coping mechanisms, which are already in place and functioning.

Market Forces, Globalization, and Violent Conflict

Soon after hostilities ceased, new secondary levels of bridging associational social capital emerged, forging the links necessary for growth and development (see Box 8). In Hargeisa, Somali private entrepreneurs (primarily from the diaspora) initiated business activities to reinstate services such as communications and public transportation, while women's groups opened markets that allowed exchange between warring clans. In Prey Koh, Cambodian transportation entrepreneurs facilitated new business ties between haulers and vegetable producers. In the immediate postconflict period, linkages external to primary groups tended to proliferate, encouraged by the potential involvement

Box 8   Market penetration and violent conflict

Cambodia

Both villages were relatively unexposed to the effects of globalization and modernization in the preconflict period. For the most part, the only external actor or influence was the government, which provided a few basic services in each village. Farming, mostly carried on by individual families, continued to be the main activity. Exchange primarily involved labor and goods, but some exchanges for money did take place.

Prasath has little economic activity except for trade within the village in local agricultural products and necessities. In general, the area had fewer resources than Prey Koh, and its proximity to a mountainous, forested region makes it more prone to surprise attacks. Prey Koh, closer to a main road and therefore to market activities, has deeper market penetration and more external ties.

Rwanda

Both Shyanda and Giti were relatively poor communes. Most types of exchange were in agricultural products and, to some extent, livestock. Scarcity of land and cattle, as well as increasing land degradation, became problems as population levels continually rose. The fall of coffee prices in the late 1980s further aggravated the worsening economic conditions. Credit, gift giving, and mutual assistance decreased as impoverishment grew.

In both communes, modernization and monetization have continued to transform forms of social capital. Heightened individualism and the increased value placed on money have led to diminishing involvement in activities to benefit the overall community and to greater reluctance to extend credit. Mutual assistance has also decreased to a degree. As money has became a more integral part of communal living, people have tended to lock up their belongings, perhaps creating a sense of mistrust or lack of security.

Guatemala

The market had little effect in either Nebaj or Puerto Barrios before the war, probably because of government policies that focused on growth and development in urban centers and did not encourage market access and development in certain rural areas. Nebaj is and has been relatively more isolated than Puerto Barrios from economic activities, except for those associated with farming.

Somalia

Economic activity has emerged in both Hargeisa and Boroma despite the conflict that continues to plague the southern regions of Somalia. Much of this new economic growth and development has taken place in communications and transportation and has been initiated by the Somali diaspora. The war actually spurred economic growth and development in the region, probably because there was less state control, less regulation, and fewer trade restrictions.

of a diaspora, the absence of state regulation and control, and the disruption of traditional constraints or of overly restrictive group loyalties.

The findings from the Rwanda and Cambodia studies suggest that modernization has also affected the transformation of the structure of social capital. Overall, local perceptions of social capital focused primarily on what was deemed "tradition" (traditional norms, values, and customs) and the social capital concepts affiliated with bonding, or primary social capital. Interviewees' definitions of social capital, for the most part, did not extend to external linkages (that is, to the state's effectiveness, capacity to function, or connectedness to the community). Participants viewed moves toward establishing linkages as a weakening of their social capital. Villagers in Prey Koh and Prasath and commune members in Giti and Shyanda all felt that market penetration and monetization had eroded local trust and mutual assistance. In other words, as they saw it, moves toward globalization had dissolved traditional social, political, and economic structures. Many stated that they thought market penetration had affected social capital in their societies more than had conflict, in terms of the shift of focus from familial and intracommunity ties to intercommunity relations.

The transformation already set in motion by trends toward globalization in each country was accelerated by conflict and the resulting break in the normal functioning of social capital systems. Oppressive and exploitative secondary relations and linkages resulted in diminished trust and weakened social cohesion. External interventions such as humanitarian relief and NGOs stepped in, to varying degrees from country to country, to fill the traditional protection and service-supplying roles typical of kin and state.

State Failure and Civil War

A lack of organizational integrity and synergy of the state, or poor vertical social capital relations, was a key cause of each conflict examined (see Box 9). In each case the government did not have the ability to perform standard state roles and was remote

Box 9 State penetration and violent conflict

Cambodia

During the conflict, state penetration was equally deep in the high-conflict village (Prey Koh) and the low-conflict village (Prasath). The state was distant from both villages in the preconflict period, providing only a few basic services to either. During the Lon Nol and Khmer Rouge regimes, the state exerted considerable pressure on communities. Many villagers were forced to join the Lon Nol ranks; some joined voluntarily for fear of being associated with the "losing" side if they did not. State power under the Khmer Rouge was absolute, and all forms of religion, culture, tradition, organization, and family were destroyed. People were herded from the cities into rural camps to work on communal farms. Punishment for any breach of conduct was severe. When the Khmer Rouge took over Prasath and Prey Koh, those who had been affiliated with the Lon Nol army were punished, and villagers were split between "old" and "new" people, according to how long they had been under Khmer Rouge control. The "old" people received privileges in preference to the "new" people, dividing the village and increasing a sense of distrust.

Rwanda

Traditionally, the central government has exerted extreme control over Rwandans.

High conflict. After the genocide erupted in Kigali and nearby areas, many Rwandans fled to Shyanda, which was known for solid Hutu and Tutsi relations. However, following a visit from the acting prime minister, sensitization sessions were held among Hutu, and killings of Tutsi began on the same day.

Low conflict. The burgomaster in Giti, unlike many communal leaders throughout Rwanda, was actually from the commune and was familiar with his constituents. When killings broke out on the edge of his commune, he united Hutu and Tutsi to safeguard Tutsi in Giti. The commune was also spared the hate politics typical throughout Rwanda from the early 1960s onward. Its shifting administrative ties with the prefectures of Kigali and Byumba weakened the chain of authority between the center and the commune, and this distance afforded Giti the space to refuse to join in the killings. In addition, Byumba was an early point of reentry for the RPF, which protected members of its ethnic group.

Guatemala

During the war, systematic violations of human rights, most of them by the state against the people, took place in both Nebaj and Puerto Barrios (as elsewhere in Guatemala). The breakdown of the legal system and of democratic controls, which allowed the violation of human rights, became a central policy of the military authorities. Often, human rights

(Box continues on next page.)

Box 9 *(continued)*

violations took the form of private violence, implemented by secret and paramilitary organizations on orders from high political figures. The violence took place away from the battlefield in most cases, striking people not directly involved in either politics or guerrilla activities.

The government had a history of repression and violence against indigenous peoples and people living in rural areas, especially if they were suspected of being affiliated with the guerrillas. Government rule enforced highly political and exclusionary economic and social policies, giving a small minority almost absolute political power and control over most resources. The government also made efforts to split communities by recruiting villagers as members of the PACs.

Somalia
Siad Barre attempted to destroy all clan-based social institutions by renaming clan leaders "peacekeepers" and incorporating them into the state bureaucracy. He attacked Somali traditions by trying to claim absolute social and political control. The regime sought to create dependence on the state in its strategy to replace the clan system. Both cities chosen for the study are in northern Somalia: Hargeisa, the capital of Somaliland, where a de facto government that provides order and services has been operating since 1991, and Boroma, which has a local government structure. Even while war continues in the rest of Somalia, some growth and development has occurred in the northern region. Since there is no central government, the legal system in both Hargeisa and Boroma is weak; thus, space for more traditional conflict-resolution mechanisms such as the use of elders as informal mediators of disputes has emerged.

---

from its constituents, whether because of anarchy or authoritarian rule (see Table 7). In Cambodia and Rwanda state penetration was sometimes ideologically driven, but its consistent goal was the retention of power by the political elite under conditions of increasing inequality, exclusion, and indignity. Both the Lon Nol and Khmer Rouge regimes were distant from their constituents yet sought to control and regulate them. In Rwanda the disconnect between the highly centralized, authoritarian government and the subjugated masses—the lack of synergy—led to the dissolution of stability and the eruption of hostilities. The Guatemalan government, plagued by corruption, was bent on retaining power and on continued exploitation and thus was highly repressive and dictatorial, with the military in the van-

CIVIC, MARKET, AND STATE ENGAGEMENT

Table 7 Organizational integrity of the state

Synergy: state and community interface	State capacity and effectiveness	
	Low	High
Low	Anarchy (collapsed states) *Somalia*	Inefficiency, ineffectiveness (weak states) *Rwanda*
High	Predation, corruption (rogue states) *Guatemala* and *Cambodia*	Cooperation, accountability, flexibility (developmental states)

Source: Based on Woolcock (1998).

guard of state penetration. A corrupt and predatory Somali state, with little connection to the local level, dissolved as a result of dysfunction, leading to armed chaos. Although the type of conflict and the indigenous manifestations of social capital were quite different in Guatemala and Somalia, lack of organizational integrity contributed to the violence in both. Relations between government and people were one-sided, with the government maintaining absolute power until warfare broke out.

The same social dynamics that enable actors to engage in integrative relations or linkages for positive outcomes can also result in the formation of groups with very negative effects, such as youth militias or, in the specific study instances, the Angka, the Interahamwe, Guatemalan PACs, and Somali renegade clans. Strong social dynamics and bonding within these groups, primarily manipulated and mobilized by the government (except in Somalia), made possible the groups' success. The negative effects of this strong perverse social capital were manifested in exclusion, hate propaganda, repression, and, eventually, slaughter.

In Cambodia after the war and in Rwanda before the war, external forces of globalization led villagers to initiate more external linkages in the course of efforts to nourish civil society. As conflict erupted in Rwanda, hate propaganda generated by the state encouraged Hutu to band together against Tutsi within their

Table 8   Intra- and extracommunity ties

Linkages (extracommunity networks)	Integration (intracommunity ties)	
	Low	High
Low	Anomie *Cambodia*	Amoral familialism *Somalia*
High	Amoral individualism *Rwanda* and *Guatemala*	Economic advancement

Source: Based on Woolcock (1998).

communities and families. Hutu power thrived on the resulting amoral individualism, which placed allegiance to the state above any community or familial loyalties. In some regions of Somalia, moves toward globalization pushed people to strengthen and increasingly depend on familial ties. In Guatemala, fierce clan alliances, combined with weak links to other communities, led to the establishment of amoral familialism and thus aggravated and perpetuated clan warfare. Solidarity among rebels and indigenous groups in Guatemala ran high, as did allegiance within the government and military to their own. Government policy acted to rupture local communities by pitting villager against villager in certain areas of the country, disrupting strong intragroup ties (see Table 8).

Thus, civic, market, and state engagement, and how it interrelated with conflict, had vast ramifications for the transformation of all four dimensions of social capital. The ideal situation is a balance between civil society and state and market penetration that nurtures primary bonds, encourages bridging, cross-cutting ties, and supports state functioning and the state's relations to its people. It is the mix of these horizontal cross-cutting ties and vertical linkages that forms the basis for true social cohesion.

Part III
From Civil War to Civil Society

6

Violent Conflict and Peacebuilding

The nature of conflict should be taken into account in shaping the structure of peacebuilding interventions (relief, reconstruction, and reconciliation) after hostilities cease. Analysis of conflict and the related coping mechanisms provide mappings of extant social capital relations and of the types of social capital that may need to be encouraged or discouraged. These insights can be an important foundation for development efforts. In addition, the political, economic, and social milieu of the postconflict country should be considered in the design of interventions. The milieu includes the stage of the local-to-global transition and its effects on power constellations, economic exchange, and social relations.

How the Nature of War Determines the Nature of Peace and Reconciliation

The conflicts that have plagued Cambodia, Rwanda, Guatemala, and Somalia have varied in duration, intensity, and nature (see Table 9). Cambodia experienced 20 years of fighting, with 4 intense years of civilian suffering at the hands of the state during the Khmer Rouge period. External warfare in Vietnam exacerbated the situation, making the country prone to sporadic bombings and invasions by foreign troops. In Rwanda, simmering tensions, beginning with the emergence of violence in 1959,

Table 9   Description of violent conflicts: four case studies

	Cambodia	Rwanda	Guatemala	Somalia
Duration	The conflict spanned two decades, divided into the Lon Nol era (1970–75), Khmer Rouge rule (1975–79), and the Heng Samrin regime (1979–89).	Sporadic hostilities have plagued Rwanda since 1959. Officially the civil war began in October 1990, with the genocide taking place from April to June 1994.	Typified by guerrilla warfare, the conflict spanned four decades, with the most intense fighting occurring during the early 1980s.	The conflict has lasted for eight years, despite numerous efforts to reach an agreement to end the fighting.
Nature	In the Lon Nol and Khmer Rouge periods, the state brutally attacked its people. Skirmishes continued in the Heng Samrin era. External and regional fighting exacerbated the situation.	The state orchestrated "ethnic" cleansing by mobilizing impoverished masses around ethnic-based hate politics. This policy led to great division at the local level, within the community, and within extended and nuclear families.	The conflict primarily took the form of guerrilla warfare, with the state mainly targeting indigenous and rural populations (those most marginalized and excluded from society). Some state mobilization at the local level did occur, dividing communities and eroding trust.	With the collapse of the government in 1991, clans began vying for power, resources, and land, wreaking havoc and chaos throughout most of Somalia. Warfare has been territorial between groups mainly aligned with clans.
Intensity	Of the 20 years of conflict, 10 years were high intensity. Communities and families were divided and forced to do hard labor. Living conditions were harsh, and torture for dissent was common. Over 2 million people died during the wars as a result of direct combat, bombing by U.S. planes, state-induced famine, torture, or disease.	Sporadic skirmishes throughout Rwanda were common after the Rwandese Patriotic Front invaded in October 1990. The genocide marked the height of the warfare, with over 800,000 people killed in three months. Tutsi men, women, and children were slaughtered with machetes, and some Hutu died in reprisal killings.	The war waxed and waned over four decades and was marked by extreme human rights violations. Massacres, disappearances, and torture were common, with the state being the main perpetrator of these actions. Government and rebel penetration within villages depleted trust within and between communities and the state.	The intensity of fighting has varied. The conflict peaked in the early 1990s. Over the past few years, fighting has dwindled, and remains confined to pockets within southern and central Somalia.

exploded in a genocide that left some 800,000 dead in a three-month period of brutal massacres. The conflict in Guatemala, typified by guerrilla warfare against a repressive state, flared up and subsided by turns for almost 40 years. Numerous human rights violations, including torture and disappearances, thoroughly dissolved trust in the state and split communities along the lines of real or perceived alliances. The dissolution of the state in Somalia as a consequence of gross misallocation of resources and power has created a vacuum in which clans vie for control of power and assets. Yet pockets of peace have emerged and Somalia has started on the road to recovery.

Despite these varying experiences with violent conflict, the roots of the conflicts have some common denominators. One underlying thread is the inequality, exclusion, and indignity that resulted as elites manipulated political, social, and economic resources to retain control during the local-to-global transition. A second similarity is the turmoil left in the wake of the transition. The combined political, social, and economic instability resulting from changes associated with this transition—from a state-centric to an open society, from traditional to national or international structures, and from a centrally planned to a market economy with increasing external market penetration—facilitated the emergence of hostilities in each country. The third commonality is the impact of the local-to-global transition on the nature and structure of social capital and the resulting social cohesion or fragmentation in each affected country.

In traditional societies, systems of economic production and exchange nurture social interactions that serve as the basis for communal social organization. Through repeated exchange at the community level, economic interaction is embedded in social relations, helping groups to cohere and imparting a sense of trust and reciprocity. As globalization, or the amalgamation of capitalism and democracy, transcends communal borders, economic interaction is disembedded from social relations through transactions that are more open and less personal. This reformation of social systems involves a shift in socioeconomic and political organization from the communal to the national or international level, transforming the structure of a traditional society's social capital base from a familial to an associational foundation. Political, economic, and social arenas expand, replacing the sense of community built on primary familial relationships with a structure of secondary associations that make up a broader civil society. Local power constellations are replaced by those at the meso or macro level. During this transformation, traditional social mechanisms for mediating conflict and peacefully reconciling differences typically become weakened, along with other traditional structures and roles.

Organizational changes, particularly as manifested in emerging market and state forces, have facilitated the expansion of economic and political interactions, creating a global interdependence that permeates even the most remote pockets of civilization. This development is increasing the pressure for nations to work within Western systems. Although capitalism and democracy may make political and economic resources more equally available and increase personal freedom and justice, the adoption of these systems, particularly the institutional underpinnings, can be slow and wrenching during periods of transformation. The confluence of tradition and modernization is turbulent, but more often than not, if it is relatively slow-moving and is effectively managed, it takes place without civil war. In some nations, however, the changes are far from peaceful. The rapid local-to-global shift creates societal fissures, alienating many people and stripping them of their identity, status, power, and access to resources. This often results in a destabilization of traditional social structures (societal fragmentation) and the creation of power vacuums in the social, economic, and political realms, ripe for exploitation and abuse (Newbury 1988).

It is against this backdrop of social, economic, and political transformation that modern violent conflicts must be viewed. Changes that have unfolded over centuries in the West have been adopted, imposed, and enforced within decades in many non-Western nations. During the Cold War, bipolar politics imposed a degree of international stabilization, but many countries still fell victim to the local-to-global transition and the associated ideological debate. Bipolar politics aggravated the conflict in Guatemala and to some extent increased the hostilities because of the political and financial support provided by the United States to a series of repressive governments. Cold War politics also gave birth to the war in Cambodia, where a severe anti-Western platform led to an extremist communist experiment that victimized millions. Somalia was also shaped by Cold War politics, as Siad Barre shifted sides between the Eastern bloc and the West, building and maximizing his means of domestic coercion through continuous militarization. After the Cold War, global cultural politics—specifically, French military assistance to the oppressive Habyarimana regime—fueled and prolonged the conflict in Rwanda.

The Effects of Globalization on Social Cohesion

The latent effects of the local-to-global transition often inadvertently nourish the seeds of inequality and exclusion already planted deep within each society by colonialism and post-independence political elites. Strong societies with inclusionary social capital—particularly as manifested in conflict-mediating institutions such as an efficient and noncorrupt bureaucracy, an independent and effective judiciary, a free press, and institutionalized modes of social insurance (safety net provisions)—are more likely to be able to prevent or withstand the socioeconomic and political shocks associated with globalization (Rodrik 1999b; Easterly 2000a, 2000b). However, as the past decade and the four case studies have demonstrated, many nations are unable to ward off hostilities, for their already underdeveloped social capital base has been further weakened by the local-to-global transition and alienated by state oppression and manipulation. As Smith and Naim observe:

> Deadly conflict has been globalized. No war, no matter how local, can be fully understood (or prevented) without looking to the local impact of global markets, the global arms trade, the transborder loyalties of kinship and tradition, the fears and interests of other people and governments, and the growing influences of nonstate participants

(whether mercenaries or Doctors Without Borders, Amnesty International or Alcoa). And just as television communicates the wickedness of war to a global audience, norms of human rights and good governance acquire a new and global authority. (Smith and Naim 2000: 21)

If globalization prepares the ground for more disparities and conflict, building cross-cutting social capital becomes even more imperative for managing and preventing conflict. Strong and effective horizontal and vertical social capital bridges groups within and between communities and links the state with a civil society that should play a role in conflict management and mediation. When that social capital is absent, conflict can escalate into violence, and society is liable to retreat into a bonded, primary survivalist mode as preexisting social cleavages are manipulated and exacerbated.

In Cambodia state actors primarily waged war against a relatively uninvolved, tradition-bound citizenry. Under the Khmer Rouge, "new" people were pitted against "old," and domination was achieved by rhetoric, fear, and coercion. Whereas ideology fueled the Cambodian conflict, identity was the driving force in Rwanda. A small elite group manipulated the masses by using the Tutsi minority as scapegoats for economic woes, transforming grievances into greed and hatred. Relations were severed between the government and communities, within communities, and in some cases within families. Social capital in both cases was manipulated and transformed to meet the political and economic needs of small groups that used to their own advantage the changes in power constellations, exchange, and social conditions brought about by globalization.

The Guatemalan state waged a vicious war against its people, primarily the politically and socioeconomically marginalized and excluded indigenous and rural populations. Government efforts, backed by external support to help crush the "communistic" guerrilla movement, split the populace through the formation of civil defense patrols (PACs), dividing communal allegiances and loyalties. These actions further eroded any horizontal ties that may have bridged Ladino and non-Ladino groups while ensuring that new linkages would not form.

Inequality and exclusion caused the collapse of the Somali government. Massive amounts of small arms and weapons on hand as a legacy of Cold War politics in the region facilitated the eruption of violent hostilities. Localized wars ravaged the country. Yet somehow, within this chaos, ministates emerged, with their own forms of government, offering services and order in the face of anarchy. In the northern region of Somalia businesses grew and developed as a result of rapid market expansion and increasing demand, with the Somali disaspora connecting local to global actors.

In each of these conflicts, the state commandeered national power and supported exclusionary and unequal political regimes. To strengthen state hegemony, government actors waged war against constituents and engaged in divisive ploys, blocking the formation of cross-cutting, bridging social capital, while utilizing instability that may have resulted from the effects of globalization to further their cause. The structure of the conflicts that ensued had ramifications for the way social capital was transformed in each country and will in turn affect future strategies for supporting social capital during reconstruction and reconciliation efforts, as well as relief delivery.

Social capital relations at the macro level (the government's ability to function and its relation to the local level) need to be addressed in postconflict peacebuilding and reconstruction measures in each of the countries studied. Institutions should serve to manage conflict by adjudicating disputes within a framework of transparent rules and procedures. Trust in the state needs to be rebuilt, and leaders will have to prove their legitimacy by instituting just and transparent political, social, and economic systems that are inclusive and participatory. State synergy, or macro-micro relations, should be an integral part of the development process. In addition, the state will need to take steps to secure itself from the shocks incurred through the globalization process and ensure that there is not a regression into conflict. Violent conflict rooted in exclusionary governance creates the very need for strategies of empowerment (Deacon 2000).

Relations between communities and between unlike or warring factions need to be established to improve the necessary linkages for economic growth and the development of civil society. Primary and secondary relations within families and communities should be nourished, even though this is the level most difficult to target from a macro perspective. If the environment for social capital is rendered conducive for the growth of civil society by allowing freedom of press, speech, and assembly, and if enough space is created to allow civil society to flourish, improved government-community relations will follow.

Because the nature and causes of war are country-specific and peculiar to each country's unique situation, efforts for relief, reconstruction, and reconciliation need to take note of these differences, acknowledge the variations in how the social fabric was damaged by each specific conflict, and assess how the social threads remaining after the conflict can be utilized to help facilitate the larger peace processes. Those dimensions that were specifically targeted and abused during conflict, whether integration, linkages, organizational integrity, or synergy, and those that emerge in response to crisis should lay the foundation for peacebuilding and sustainable development.

7

Policies and Programs for Strengthening Social Capital and Social Cohesion

Social capital can take many forms and serve diverse functions, depending on its nature and use. It can contribute to social cohesion or spur social fragmentation. It can be a source of mutual aid and protection in the face of violent conflict, or, just as readily, it can be perverted to mobilize unemployed youth into militia and bring about horrendous acts of genocide. Social capital can help bridge and mitigate the exclusive relations that create the conditions for conflict, or it can reinforce highly exclusionary bonds such as those that exist within gangs or extremist ethnic groups. It can substitute for state and market failures or complement their provision of basic protection or safety nets.

Thus, social capital is a double-edged sword with regard to conflict and development. Violent conflict can destroy primary bonds, undercutting indigenous social capital as a form of social protection. But by weakening such primary bonds, conflict can create opportunities for bridges to other networks and can displace relations that tend to build dependency, limit access to new information and opportunities, and retard change. Under such conditions, social capital can serve as a key source of reconciliation and reconstruction in divided societies through the formation of broad and diverse networks. The development of civic

cut across traditional bonding social capital to
crossing ethnic, religious, age, income, and gen-
vide the basis for the mediation, conflict-management, and conflict-resolution mechanisms that all societies
require to sustain peace and development. Finally, a new government presents the opportunity to improve government ability and deepen community relations. For development assistance
to be successful, it must focus on building such social capital as
an integral part of any conflict-prevention measure or people-
centered reconstruction effort.

Numerous policy and operational recommendations for international actors concerned about strengthening social cohesion by building social capital can be drawn from the four
country studies. This chapter presents recommendations for
specific interventions geared toward each state. (For further
discussion see Martin 1996b; Adam and Ford 1998; Uvin 1998;
Nee 2000.)

Cambodia: Nurturing Associations for Economic Growth and Development

The destruction of the Cambodian social fabric caused by the
various conflicts is tragic and has had devastating effects, yet the
communities have remained resilient even while in exile in refugee camps in neighboring countries. Reconstruction efforts should
build on the existing primary relations and coping mechanisms
that emerged during the war. External interventions should seek
to facilitate additional linkages geared toward economic growth
and development and to intensify civic engagement among
groups and between local groups, the government, and market
forces.

Attempts to support cooperation, participation, and group
solidarity may not be immediately appropriate during initial
development efforts. The dissolution of trust within Cambodian
society was a direct consequence of the societal fragmentation
brought about by the Lon Nol government and by the Khmer
Rouge's campaign to manipulate people and retain control

through coercion, suspicion, and fear. In the postwar era, if this lack of trust is not acknowledged and addressed, true reconstruction cannot take place. Until trust is rebuilt, attempts to encourage solidarity and group cooperation may backfire by reminding Cambodians of the Khmer Rouge's communal works and the collectivism of the *krom Samaki* under the Heng Samrin regime (Nee 1995). External interventions must be sensitive to these matters and allow cooperation to occur spontaneously, supporting efforts that create networks among people and build a responsive and responsible civil society.

Efforts to encourage participation by convening meetings in villages may be inadvertently counterproductive. Villagers may attend meetings, but often they do so because of perceived coercion, not out of free will. Meetings called by external actors are reminiscent of Pol Pot days, when villagers expected to listen to political propaganda, not participate. Furthermore, these types of meeting tend to alienate the poor, who spend the meeting thinking how they will get their next meal and resent this use of their time (Nee 1995). Ownership of initiatives is critical to building sustainable cross-cutting social capital.

Development organizations need to recognize and act on such threats to social capital as acute poverty, increasing population pressure, degradation of resources, and the emergence of a market economy in the absence of appropriate regulation, the rule of law, and safety nets for poor households. Any external development efforts in these areas should be designed to enhance the state's capacity and its ability to relate to citizens and communities in a democratic manner.

Overall, Cambodians lack the economic and social infrastructure needed to crack the shell of poverty. To build this infrastructure, community participation and grassroots institutions are needed, but for the most part, these features are absent in Cambodian society. Both could be facilitated by the strong presence of secondary social capital linkages. Decentralization, local ownership, and participation work only if communities are socially cohesive, appropriately organized, and democratic. Development actors should capitalize on the existing pagoda networks, which are organized and cohesive. Self-help groups are also increasing in popularity and number (Cambodia 1999).

Current forms of social capital related to the village economy ensure basic survival and a livelihood for some people (social protection) and allow exploitation of people and resources by others. Extant social capital should be encouraged to mature into a more responsible management of available resources, based on principles of equity and sustainability. If possible, development actors should avoid or minimize interventions that reinforce the negative elements of existing social capital. This implies shunning efforts that focus on vertical planning without putting in place accompanying horizontal structures and accountability to lower levels. Currently, it is more important to strengthen Cambodia's horizontal social capital, encompassing both familial and associational relations, than to focus on vertical social capital such as efforts to strengthen government capacity—although work in this area is also needed, particularly in efforts to eliminate corruption and build justice and democracy.

The current role of social capital in the realm of social services and welfare is geared toward meeting the community's own needs, but to a very small and inadequate extent. External agencies must step in to supplement this role and, in the process, allow social capital to effectively use and shape services, moving from social protection to service delivery. The United Nations Development Programme's Carrere Project and the World Bank–financed Northeast Village Development Project (NVDP) are good examples of efforts to build local capacity and social capital into the development process. (See Box 10 for details on the NVDP.) These are second-generation community fund or social development approaches in which community resources are managed, not through intermediary agents but by the village itself, building on existing institutions and relations and creating new ones. The goal is to connect to markets and create a form of social capital that arises from community traditions and cultural and familial solidarity but that also involves people of diverse backgrounds in numerous overlapping and reinforcing relationships created by repeated and predictable economic and social exchanges.

Box 10   Using decentralization and participation to target the rural poor in Cambodia

A number of rural development projects have been initiated in Cambodia during the reconciliation and reconstruction period that began in 1992, and they have had a positive, although limited, impact. A top priority of the current national development strategy is to spread the benefits of development more widely to rural areas, where 90 percent of poor households live. To date, the Cambodian government and its responsible line agencies have had little on-the-ground experience with planning, managing, and coordinating rural development projects. The development objective of the Northeast Village Development Project (NVDP) is to introduce decentralized, participatory, poverty reduction–oriented rural development approaches in some of the poorest areas of Cambodia and to provide the government with experience in managing such programs. Experience of this kind will be needed to formulate and carry out a cohesive national strategy for rural development. The NVDP will also widen the World Bank's experience in dealing with decentralized, participatory projects.

By targeting institutional, social, and economic issues, the NVDP will attempt to enhance rural development and natural resource management, improve human resources, reduce poverty, and strengthen institutional capacity. In addition, the NVDP is designed to increase the capacity of provincial government offices to help local communities plan and manage small rural development subprojects. Local commune development committees will be expected to take on an increased local government role, assisted by working systems and trained personnel, in carrying out participatory rural appraisal. The project will help provide people in the area with community investments needed to improve their incomes. Through participation in village development committees, the poorest households will be able to make their needs known. Opportunities will be created for local NGOs and contractors to develop activities in the area.

The goal of the NVDP is to help reaffirm Cambodians' trust in the government and enhance the government's legitimacy while increasing its organizational integrity. Through decentralization, the government will nurture more synergistic relations with rural communities, further ameliorating its relations with the villages. Participation in the development process will build local capacity, help strengthen bridging and bonding social capital ties, improve local conflict-resolution mechanisms, and strengthen faith and trust in the government.

Source: World Bank (1999).

Rwanda: Rebuilding Family, Community, and State Interrelations

Since the end of the war in Rwanda, the government has made great strides toward reconciling groups and taking initiatives to encourage growth and development. However, much work remains to be done: the country is impoverished, and Rwandans openly assert that justice toward those responsible for the genocide has not been carried out. Although Hutu and Tutsi have banded together to rebuild their lives, they do not have a great deal of trust in each other. Recommendations from the study include improving the state's organizational integrity, linkages, and, most important, synergy with the community level. A priority in social capital development in Rwanda must be to dilute the potency of ethnic, tribal, and religious identities by creating meaningful relations among individuals, civil society organizations, and the state.

Owing to the perceived ineffectiveness of the International Criminal Tribunal for Rwanda and the common view that it will be unable to administer justice, efforts have been made to reinstate *gacaca*, a traditional system of justice exercised by a group of community elders, to help process genocide crimes. The specifics of how this mechanism would work in conjunction with the tribunal are still under discussion. Many Rwandans see this procedure as the only hope for reconciliation, and it would provide a much-needed venue for both Hutu and Tutsi to relate their experiences and voice their concerns. International actors should find some means of supporting this process—but with caution. Elders and sages chosen from the commune may be better able to handle rulings and sentencing of the *génocidaires*, since they know the situation and the people firsthand. There is, however, a danger of subjective rulings and inability to conduct fair trials in certain communes. Nevertheless, attempts should be made to seek individual accountability, thus helping to diminish the tendency to ascribe collective guilt to all Hutu (Des Forges 1999).

As in Cambodia, there was much sensitivity to the manipulation of traditional collective action—in this case *umuganda*, or traditional cooperative labor, which had been transformed into forced labor and which many felt had been perverted by the Habyarimana regime. Trust in collective organs such as cooperatives will have to be gradually built from the ground up so that these organs are seen as "people's cooperatives" that the people themselves, rather than the government, initiated.

Another key factor in the reconstruction of intra- and inter-community relations is the establishment of a free and objective media. The genocide was able to spread so quickly and effectively because of propaganda issued by biased, extremist radio programs, journals, and weekly papers. Efforts to ensure effective and fair media may help prevent a recurrence of violence by linking Hutu and Tutsi once again in a cohesive Rwandan identity and may thus help hold the government accountable.

Efforts to build civil society in Rwanda failed in the past, as the rapid explosion of genocidal killings showed. Many groups and organizations supported by international agencies failed because these efforts were overfunded, too rapidly created, and artificially imposed and had poor information networks and accountability (Uvin 1998). Facilitating the creation of NGOs is not just a matter of freeing the space necessary for their existence but also of using these groups to go beyond the boundaries of family, ethnic group, and location as the basis for group cohesion. The state—authoritarian and permeating most aspects of civil society—was unable to operate in a democratic, inclusive manner. Social learning and social change, not just the presence of numerous types of organizations, are required to make up a healthy civil society.

The process of developing social capital within communities and between constituents and the state takes a long time. It must be initiated internally, and it requires a gradual increase in the ability and willingness to shape the political sphere. Pluralism and democracy must be promoted along with social capital initiatives. Through this process, people gain confidence in their ability to operate within the public arena. As society becomes more open, networks of communication and cooperation arise between and among communities, while divisions based on ethnicity, religion, gender, and region are overcome. Knowledge of politics and political workings increase, as do skills in conflict mediation, compromise, and negotiation. This type of growth requires space and time, neither of which was available in Rwanda. The way civil society emerged earlier in Rwanda, almost wholly guided by external mechanisms and goals, most likely hurt rather than helped social and political growth and development. Because civil society groups were not held accountable for promoting democratization, their existence often worsened rather than improved Hutu-Tutsi relations. Civil society's strong links and ties to the government meant that what did develop in Rwanda was rather exclusive (Uvin 1998).

Projects that decentralize state power and increase participation by civil society actors and individuals should be implemented to help rebuild faith in the central government and encourage cooperation among constituents. Community-driven reconstruction approaches such as the World Bank Community Reintegration and Development Project (described in Box 11) are attempting to create the space for development of social capital that can transcend "ethnic" lines through increased participation and that not only unite groups within communities but also link communities to the state through decentralization. Joint community decisionmaking to assess and prioritize community needs and determine and manage the allocation of resources to address these needs can be a powerful source of reconciliation through reconstruction. One main goal is to build local institutions that promote inclusive development by giving people a voice and that are capable of creating the social infrastructure necessary for conflict mediation.

Guatemala and Somalia: Improving State Capacity and Civil Society

The conflicts in Guatemala and Somalia inflicted much damage on the structure, legitimacy, and credibility of the state. Policies for rebuilding social capital in each country should focus first on improving the state's ability to function and on clearly delineating its role. The rehabilitation of the state can then serve as the foundation for the further development of civil society actors and the building of cross-cutting ties between clans (Somalia) and

Box 11   Building trust to rebuild Rwanda

This is the first time that we are asked what we need. If this is the approach this government is taking, we will finally be able to develop our country.
A community elder, on the Community Reintegration and Development Project

Since coming to power, and particularly since the massive return of refugees in 1996–97, Rwanda's Government of National Unity has faced regional security issues that have hindered peaceful development. To dismantle the legacy of centralized decisionmaking, the government initiated an inclusive community-level approach to development. This approach is designed to involve Rwandans closely in the management of their own affairs and to give local administrative structures the primary responsibility for development activities.

The World Bank's Community Reintegration and Development Project (CRDP), approved in December 1998, supports this approach. It assists war-affected communities, returned nationals, and other vulnerable groups through community-based reconstruction, reintegration, and development, and it strengthens the capacity of communities and local and national administrations to implement development subprojects. The CRDP focuses on three tasks: transferring decisionmaking and expenditure authority from the central to the community level; building partnerships between local administrations and local populations for sectoral planning and project implementation; and building trust and cooperation within and between local government and the local population.

The CRDP was prepared with the participation of local communities. It fully involves the national government while ensuring that subprojects are chosen, implemented, and evaluated locally. This approach is expected to improve effectiveness and sustainability by increasing both government and local support. The project will empower rural populations to make choices, increase self-reliance, revitalize local economies, and bring communities together through local decisionmaking on and involvement in development activities or subprojects.

The CRDP is supported by a US$5 million learning and innovation credit, a new Bank lending instrument designed to test on a small scale the feasibility of a larger project. The project is being implemented in 12 communes with a combined population of approximately 500,000. If successful, it will be replicated elsewhere in the country, helping to build a more peaceful Rwanda.

Source: World Bank (1998).

between indigenous and rural groups and Ladinos (Guatemala). Governments founded on transparency, accountability, and democratic principles will be able to make greater headway in social and economic growth and development. In Guatemala this process is well under way. In Somalia there is no official state government, but de facto governments do exist in the northern regions, and success in these areas may pave the way for stability in the rest of Somalia.

Social capital policies and projects should strive to build linkages among communities and between communities and the government. The Guatemalan government and the local governments in northern Somalia should focus on increasing the number of actors in civil society and should especially support those actors that adhere to ideals of equality and inclusion. Increased support should therefore be given to growing enterprises and for-profit actors in social initiatives. In addition, horizontal networks between different types of actors should be created. Training for government representatives in partnership skills and use of the media to provide information on civil society will also help further intercommunity and government-community relations. Normative obstacles that impede the development of social capital can be reduced by conflict-resolution initiatives, such as lobbying for legislative reform, developing formal understandings between civil society actors and the government, and simplifying bureaucratic procedures. A thriving civil society may emerge as a result of government support for an increase in the weight, diversity, and quality of civil society actors, along with improvement of local opportunities and confidence in social relations.

Most development efforts in Guatemala have been aimed at improving the state's capacity and effectiveness. Policies in support of society's efforts to raise revenues, control social risks, reduce poverty, and provide social protection to citizens will help strengthen primary levels of social capital (see Box 12). Policies that support community empowerment and productive initiatives may be considered to support secondary social capital. Thus, there are two distinct spheres of action: welfare economic policies and social development policies.

Box 12 Institutional development and strengthening: the indigenous women's defensoria in Guatemala

Historically, indigenous women in Guatemala have suffered twofold discrimination: as indigenous people and as women. They were particularly vulnerable during the internal violent conflict. To address these issues, the government of Guatemala established the Office for the Defense of Indigenous Women's Rights (Defensoria) under the Presidential Office for Human Rights (COPREDEH). This was the first postconflict initiative in Guatemala to incorporate indigenous participation into the management and administration of a public institution.

The main objectives of the Defensoria are to (a) assist in the development of public policies and programs aimed at preventing and defending against discrimination and at abolishing all forms of violence against indigenous women; (b) provide social services and legal advice to women victims of violence, discrimination, sexual harassment, and other violations of their rights; (c) design, coordinate, and implement training programs and disseminate information on indigenous women's rights; and (d) propose legal reforms regarding indigenous women's rights.

To carry out these tasks, the Defensoria will have a national office and eight regional offices managed and administered by indigenous women; a consultative council composed of representatives of the 24 indigenous linguistic communities of Guatemala; a coordinating council made up of members of the main indigenous women's organizations; and an interinstitutional commission that includes as members the vice-ministers who will implement the recommendations of the Defensoria in each ministry.

This project will promote the inclusion of one of Guatemala's most excluded groups and will build indigenous women's capacity to interface with external actors and represent their own interests. It will improve social capital both within the group and between the group and government offices.

It is more difficult to forecast how state formation may evolve in Somalia. However, it is clear that the penetration of market forces, especially in Hargeisa, has created a broadly networked associational form of social capital that has served the community well in the process of reconciliation and reconstruction. By contrast, in areas where market penetration is limited and traditional clan structures control associational behavior, hopes for transcending the situation of violent conflict appear dim.

Much of the support given to Somalia to rebuild social capital and facilitate reconstruction should be focused on the emerging economic sector. Trade between regions in Somalia is developing, and exports of traditional products such as livestock and bananas are increasing. Mobility is not directly hindered: airlines are operating, and fuel for airplanes is available. Communications are functioning, financial transfers are possible, and consumer goods and food are on hand. Thus, efforts should be directed toward supporting the further development of linkages or externally oriented secondary relations, which will help the economic sector expand. Meanwhile, political institutions have emerged, primarily at the local level. International efforts to support indigenous institutions, or the revival of Somali government capacity and community relations, should encourage these institutions to develop spontaneously as long as they are pluralistic, inclusionary, and tolerant (Adam and Ford 1998).

Although many international actors have attempted to initiate peacemaking in Somalia, lasting peace will have to come about as a result of internal desire and capacity, as in Guatemala, where women's groups acted as a catalyst in the peace process. In the past, external influences have caused major problems within Somalia, despite good intentions. For example, Cold War politics fostered a focus on military development, resulting in a force of 120,000 soldiers for a nation with 7 million–8 million people. One could also argue that since the conflict began, external aid has exacerbated the situation instead of providing relief. Many donor payments meant to buy protection for aid deliveries instead went to purchase arms (Adam and Ford 1998).

Donors seek to encourage Somali groups to come together in some unitary structure, at least partly because it is easier to deal with a single entity than with competing factions. This goal may be understandable and logical, but it may be that donor-driven attempts to bring unity have actually increased fragmentation; linking international promises of aid to unitary governance has increased the amount of spoils to be won through competition.

Box 13   Women, grassroots movements, and peace initiatives in Somalia

The dissolution of the state and the disappearance of state services in Somalia have ignited much community development action on the local level. These grassroots movements not only strive to provide services but also facilitate trade and the promotion of human rights and democracy. More often than not, the efforts have been initiated by women, who have been empowered as a result of the conflict in Somalia and who also play a natural role as peacemakers.

Somali society practices exogamy; a women leaves her family and home to marry into another clan. Somali women, with no clan of their own, have traditionally mediated and mitigated conflicts between their husbands' and fathers' clans. This cultural practice has made conflict mediation among clans a natural progression for many women. The hardships of war have also forced women to become more responsible for their own and their families' livelihoods. Many men have been lost in the fighting, and women have picked up the burden of the men's home responsibilities while keeping up with their own duties. Perhaps peace efforts looking to long-term solutions should focus more on grassroots women's movements than on male political leaders.

Recent workshops held by the Center for the Strategic Initiatives of Women have brought together women from many different clans in Somalia. Through the sharing of common warfare experiences, the women have become even more united across clan lines in their efforts for peace. An example of their resolve is the "Green-Line" market activities, in which Somali women cross over into other clans' territories to exchange goods and discuss peace initiatives. External efforts to make peace in Somalia must learn to focus on bottom-up methods that assist grassroots movements (which are primarily headed by women), offer support to areas that have already achieved peace, and work on isolating destabilizing elements such as the warlord mafiosos who have blocked peace movements out of fear of losing money, power, and status (Prendergast and Bryden 1999).

General recommendations for intervention in Somalia include improving donor collaboration in support of local autonomy; establishing a power-sharing structure that helps decentralize power; encouraging increased roles for women (see Box 13); using Islam as a means to unite the people and to establish institutions for building civil society; encouraging a free and unregulated market economy; creating space for local adaptations of external technologies and management systems; making use of traditional institutions for land management, conflict mediation, and legal adjudication; supporting a free press; and improving and nurturing regional links to enhance security in the Horn of Africa (Adam and Ford 1998).

8

Harnessing Social Capital and Social Cohesion to Prevent Violent Conflict

The interface of social capital with the integration of vertical and horizontal relations and cross-cutting, bridging ties determines levels of social cohesion and a society's capacity to manage conflict. True social cohesion reflects a society with the means to withstand internal and external shocks while successfully managing diversity and conflicting interests within the country. As evidenced in the case studies, there are three main mechanisms that can hinder or encourage the eruption of hostilities: policies, markets, and civil society. These mediating mechanisms help shape the social relations of a society, both informally and formally. They have the potential to destroy or build communities and to fuel or defuse violent conflict. Peter Berger has observed,

> In the new political era, the cultural resources that lead to social cohesion and the limits of that cohesion in our societies are of the utmost importance. It will be the primary task of societies to promote social cohesion as the basic source of economic development and ecological sensibility (Berger 1998).

Mediating Mechanisms: Policies, Markets, and Civil Society

Policies. In general, state policies (or, for that matter, the policies and programs of international agencies or NGOs) for supporting social capital should parallel the basic precepts established for good governance. That is, they should be inclusive, equitable, and empowering. If they are not, state policies can descend into state-driven warfare. The example of Rwanda, where state policies—on citizens' rights, property, educational access, and employment in the civil service—were geared toward isolating and marginalizing the Tutsi illustrates all too well how policies can divide communities and lead to violent conflict.

When pursuing postconflict development or recovery, governments should not rush economic reform policies to meet outside expectations, for that could divert attention from the more critical task of building government institutions, the rule of law, democratic rights, and social safety nets based on the restoration of sound relationships (social capital). The timing and sequencing of policy reform are critical. Economic policy reform without attendant creation of institutional capacity and reform of social policy can only foment social fragmentation and the recurrence of violent conflict. It will be necessary to carefully shape the formation of policies at the top and social practices at the bottom (connecting the macro with the micro level). The aim is for these levels to reinforce one another and work toward mending the social fabric, slowly reversing ingrained hatred and assisting in the healing and formation of trust as an indispensable ingredient in a nation's cohesiveness, stability, and economic development. The admonition to "get the policies right" may still be valid, but it is not sufficient. "Getting the social relations right" is necessary for avoiding violent conflict.

Development organizations, whether involved in conflict prevention or in reconstruction efforts, should adopt policies that help strengthen and rebuild responsive vertical social capital at the state level, in terms of that state's capabilities, role, and links to communities. Such policies include establishing impartiality while maintaining a do-no-harm mentality, investing in organizations of the poor, and providing incentives for good governance by encouraging positive political reform to reduce inequity and to improve basic services, the rule of law, and political and economic participation. Rodrik's (1999b) research, buttressed by others (Rodriguez 1977; Shah 1998; Easterly 1999), has empirically demonstrated that countries which experience sharp drops in growth are those with divided societies (as measured by such indicators as inequality and ethnic fragmentation) and lacking in the fundamental institutions necessary to mediate conflict—an efficient, noncorrupt bureaucracy, an independent judiciary, a free press, and a vibrant civil society.

State policies that are blind to social analysis—policies that reduce subsidies to the vulnerable in the aftermath of war, privatize state assets into an institutional vacuum, raise taxes regressively, reduce or increase subsidies in favor of one or another group, downsize an already underpaid or unpaid civil service or army, and repatriate refugees or demobilize combatants without the capacity or resources to provide a transitional safety net or employment-generating opportunities—are high-risk ventures. As Story (1998) noted in summing up experience with structural adjustment and ethnicity in Rwanda, the critical factors are the extent to which economic differentiation and competition are "ethnicized" and the impact of adjustment is mediated through (and possibly reinforcing) divisions associated with particular ethnic groups. Although the Rwandan genocide cannot be attributed to adjustment policies per se, a lesson that can be drawn from the experience is that a people's expectations of how adjustment will affect them is as important as the eventual impact itself. A climate of economic uncertainly kindled by the memory of historical injustices can readily shape present-day fears, setting the stage for violent conflict.

Markets. The penetration of markets into society can foster secondary networks of social capital. In northern Somalia, globalization, in the form of external market penetration and the spread of knowledge, information, and technology, has facilitated peace efforts by enabling exchange and economic growth despite adverse conditions. The connectivity of the Somalia diaspora, easy access to ports, telecommunications, and access to capital (through electronic transmittal of remittances) have all facilitated this growth, linked groups within the northern region, and created new social and economic bridges. Weak state penetration (especially in Hargeisa) has also enabled this development of market forces, removing the threat of overregulation and an inefficient bureaucracy. The drive of the market has helped form cross-cutting links in northern Somalia and encourage governmental and institutional (civil society) development, which have reinforced each other as potential conflict-mediating mechanisms. By contrast, we have seen how market isolation in Prey Koh, Cambodia, has reinforced inward-looking bonds and a general lack of social capacity to compete in the marketplace, sometimes leading to a widening of the gap between rich and poor through exploitation rather than development. Improving the quality of a community's social capital and its ability to deal confidently with changing market access during transition can be critical to the development of the community.

Civil society. An active civil society that protects the rights of the individual and of groups while engaging and holding the state accountable to the rule of law is another important mediating force. As some observers note, Cambodia today has only moved from a war without justice to a peace without justice. Years of factional war, a heavily armed populace, a corrupt judiciary and police force, and an inefficient bureaucracy all contribute to a culture in which violence is still the preferred way of getting things done (Faulder 2000).

The Pol Pot regime purposely destroyed Cambodian civil society in an attempt to erase all forms of traditional bonds, from kinship to religion and the arts, and to destroy modern bridges by targeting professionals such as teachers and doctors. A perverted bonding form of social capital emerged in the form of the Angka, "The Organization," which consisted of a formerly excluded group—semiliterate, unemployed youths—led by a handful of extremist intellectuals (who had also been excluded). The Angka perpetrated one of the cruelest genocides in modern history. Trust between individuals virtually disappeared as people were reduced to spying and informing on one another and to obeying the rules without question. The common saying then was, "If you want to survive, you must pretend to be deaf and mute" (Nee 2000).

The combined effects of centuries of feudalism and militarism have left Cambodian communities with weak social links. Some students of Cambodian village life even question whether Cambodian villages may be regarded as communities in a real sense (Vijghen and others 1966; Ebihara 1976). The breakdown of basic community values, norms, and social relationships and the ongoing social violence have virtually destroyed social cohesion in Cambodia. Under such circumstances, people tend to take care of themselves rather than think of others. The task ahead is to revitalize the functioning of existing social structures, incorporating them into the mainstream of development by empowering people to participate in decisions about their own communities' needs, resources, and actions—in short, building a civil society capable of mediating between individuals, groups, and the state.

The media can help civil society to thrive. A free press enables public expression and informs the public of government actions. During the genocide in Rwanda, the media, instead of defusing conflict, ignited and inflamed ethnic hatred. State radio and television went so far as to broadcast lists of Hutu in each commune who had not participated in the killings, thereby publicly pressuring them to join the genocide.

By contrast, the nonprofit organization Search for Common Ground, which works for societal conflict resolution in the United States and elsewhere, is using the media to build bridging ties in Rwanda's neighbor, Burundi. There too, animosities between Hutu and Tutsi have led to thousands of deaths, and hate radio has been used to incite ethnic violence. In 1995, Search for Common Ground launched Studio Ijambo ("wise words," in Kirundi) as a radio production center where Hutu and Tutsi journalists work together to provide balanced news, features, and even soap operas. The studio is located in the country's capital, Bujumbura. Since, as a listener survey indicated, 99.98 percent of Burundians consider themselves to be regular radio listeners, this medium is an important means of counteracting hate propaganda with a message of understanding and reconciliation.[9]

In societies in transition from violent conflict to peace and from crisis to sustainable development, the transformation of social capital that strengthens social cohesion can play a critical role in the transition from welfare-oriented, protectionist relief to an activist development orientation. State policies, markets, and civil society can all contribute to or detract from this process. In this perspective, communities are viewed not just as victims with needs but as survivors with capacities.

Ensuring Human Security: Managing Conflict by Connecting and Empowering People

In Rwanda, in a stark example of social capital gone awry, Hutu elite were able to mobilize exclusionary and divisive social capital that bonded Hutu—primarily male unemployed and uneducated youth—into such groups as the Interahamwe. While some Hutu willingly participated in the massacres, others were ordered or forced to kill. Within Hutu extremism, bonding, exclusive social capital powered the groups' success by providing excellent information networks and a sense of solidarity, obligation, and civic duty. But social capital can also form bridges, enabling cross-cutting and inclusive ties, such as those among the indigenous Guatemalan women's groups that have united to sustain peace efforts. For example, see Box 12 in chapter 7, which described the formation of the Office for the Defense of Indigenous Women's Rights (Defensoria), the first postconflict initiative in Guatemala to incorporate indigenous participation into the management and administration of a public institution. The creation of links between excluded groups and government offices is an example of the optimal application and use of social capital stocks.

What conditions reinforce exclusionary bonding social relations, and what conditions nurture inclusionary bridging social relations? How can societies cope with normative conflicts under conditions of pluralism and diversity? How does the ebb and flow of social capital work to hold a society together or fragment it? These critical questions are key to understanding the role of social capital in promoting social cohesion and conflict management as a basic source of economic development and human progress. Connecting, empowering, and integrating people and organizations are basic transformative actions that emerge from our analysis to shed light on these questions.

Connections. Physical rehabilitation and reconstruction hinge on social reconciliation, which successfully connects adversarial groups. In Rwanda, for example, since the end of the genocide attempts have been made to place Hutu in government positions to balance political power. Meanwhile, space has been created for the reemergence of civil society actors. Yet the new social fabric of Rwanda is complicated, with subgroups and schisms that will take generations to heal. Cross-cutting social capital needs to be nurtured to link not just Hutu and Tutsi but also those within subgroups. But hope prevails as associations of widows and female heads of households bridge ethnic lines to form new social capital.

In northern Somalia, the diaspora has facilitated not only an economic connectedness to global markets, but has transformed social relationships among local clans by strengthening cross-cutting ties through market transactions and open channels of communication.

Empowerment. Decentralization and participation can empower people to take over development and give them a sense of control over their future. To dismantle the legacy of centralized decisionmaking and begin to forge these bridging links, the Rwandan government initiated an inclusive community-driven approach to development founded on the concepts of participation and decentralization. This approach is designed to involve Rwandans closely in the management of their own affairs and to give local administrative structures the primary responsibility for development activities, thus not only empowering the groups but also encouraging them to work together to build their connected futures.

Efforts by international actors to build and strengthen civil society must be accompanied by efforts to improve respect for pluralism, tolerance, and participatory, democratic principles. Equality among social groups that promotes ties cutting across ethnicity, clans, gender, age, religion, and political ideologies is necessary if quality civic engagement is to flourish. Such civil society binds together potentially disintegrative elements, building new, cohesive social identities while keeping bonding elements of communal identity in balance.

While cross-cutting ties are being established, assessments must also be made of existing bonding social capital bases, and care must be taken that external efforts do not erode them. Once these local coping mechanisms are identified, they must be incorporated into the reconstruction process. External interventions need to be sensitive to indigenous organizations and be careful not to wipe out the groups' own efforts and their tendencies toward self-reliance. Rather, they should strengthen indigenous capacities, especially to bridge to new roles, functions, and relationships. International actors should ensure that their development efforts do not nurture or encourage dependency through the manner in which leadership, money, know-how, or materials are provided. Local actors should not be inadvertently undercut by external funding for government projects already being handled locally. Development actors must be careful not to undermine confidence in internal and external coping mechanisms; they should nurture these mechanisms' capacity to handle and, in fact, lead efforts toward change. External intervention should not become a disincentive to self-help, nor should project design and implementation weaken the authority and prestige of local leaders. Donor efforts should seek to go beyond the precept of "do no harm" to "do some good," enhancing community self-esteem and self-reliance through the development of social capacity for informal participation and collective action.

The goal of building capacity at the local level should be to improve access to information and transparency in decisionmaking and to enhance local leaders' skills in obtaining information, empowering decisionmaking, building local alliances, resolving conflicts, and implementing projects so as to facilitate decentralization efforts. Care must be taken that development or relief efforts at the local level do not obscure underlying political realities and unintentionally mask contradictions and inadequacies within the society. In hostile environments, extant social capital bases should be used for peacebuilding initiatives, and positive information should be provided to groups under stress to dispel negative, hate-filled propaganda. (The World Bank's Rwanda Community Reintegration and Development Project is an example of a constructive approach; see Box 11 in chapter 7.)

Building Resilient Communities: Integrating Relief and Development

Building resilient communities in the wake of violent conflict is essential to sustainable peace and development. Integration can occur on many levels, from the cooperation of diverse groups in strengthening social capital and constructing civil society to the integration of states and citizens through markets and policies—all playing their respective roles in transforming social capital and enhancing enduring social cohesion.

During the postconflict period, when a transition from initial humanitarian relief to longer-term development takes place, the integration of policies and operations occurs on many different levels, with varying success. Government actors, as well as external international organizations (such as business persons, donors, and NGOs) are typically involved in one way or another in the relationship between humanitarian relief and development and thus play a key role in helping to integrate activities.

It is becoming increasingly clear that relief agencies must focus more on sustainable solutions, taking a development-oriented approach to the provision of humanitarian assistance, while development agencies need to help remedy the deficiencies (in, for example, political will, financing, knowledge, and organization) in the transition from relief to development. On the basis of studies examining social capital, two primary recommendations emerge that could help improve the strategies and operations of both international actors.

1. *Relief should not strengthen bonding associations at the expense of building bridging networks.* All too often, relief inadvertently fuels conflict and reinforces undemocratic processes, particularly when access and goods (food) become instruments of war (Goodhand and Hulme 1999). Humanitarian actors, while supporting primary relations, can act to stifle, or at least do not encourage, the development of the links and ties necessary to progress to more sustainable development. If not carefully implemented, relief can strengthen primary social capital and yet prevent reconciliation by strengthening exclusionary bonding ties. Relief can cater to individual rather than community needs, thus lessening social cohesion and, consequently, group trust, norms of reciprocity, and solidarity. Relief can keep people alive, but in worst-case scenarios it can unintentionally promote polarization and more conflict (Box 14).

The real challenge in the transition is the fine balance between saving lives and providing sustainable livelihoods that consciously creates bridging social capital while providing relief and rehabilitation. It is not enough to provide food; doing so can subtly build dependence and a sense of entitlement. Agencies must work to empower the victims to take back their own lives and become active producers of food again, building a sense of self-reliance and responsibility. Repatriation of refugees without social and economic reintegration and without providing opportunities for mutual understanding, learning, and earning is a recipe for further impoverishment. Emergency drugs and medical treatment in the absence of health services and social security may sustain life but will not end suffering. The creation of sustainability that prevents dependence stems from the emergence of bridging linkages, which unite disparate communities in efforts for social and economic growth and development.

Humanitarian and development actors should jointly assess existing bonding social capital bases and take care that their external efforts do not erode them nor blindly reinforce them at the expense of facilitating cross-cutting ties. Social assessment or conflict analysis, including the explicit recognition of underlying societal cleavages as sources of social conflict and tension, should be a core aspect of preparing for assistance. Such analysis should

---

Box 14   Relief and the perpetuation of violent conflict

Shortly after the genocide in Rwanda, refugee camps in Zaire were plagued with large numbers of génocidaires who used innocent Hutu masses as shields from Rwanda Patriotic Front forces bent on retribution and international actors concerned with punishing the egregious human rights abuses of the genocide. Besides providing a stable environment and shelter, humanitarian agencies kept Hutu Power members well fed. Malnutrition rates in the camps were far lower than anywhere else in the region—on a par, in fact, with those in Western Europe. General medical care was also equal to the best available in central Africa. People living near the camps spoke enviously of refugee entitlements, and several said they had pretended to be refugees to gain admission to camp clinics. According to Gourevitch (1998: 270–71):

> After having all essential living expenses covered by charity, camp residents were free to engage in commerce, and aid agencies frequently provided enticements—like agricultural supplies—to do so. The major camps in Zaire quickly became home to the biggest, best-stocked, and cheapest markets in the region. Zaireans came for miles to shop *chez les Rwandais*, where at least half the trade appeared to be in humanitarian-aid stuffs—beans, flour, and oil, spilling from sacks and tins stamped with the logos of foreign donors. And, as the Interahamwe and ex-FAR [soldiers of the former government army] stepped up their attacks on the Tutsi herdsmen of North Kivu, the Goma camp markets became famous for incredibly cheap beef. (165–66)
>
> Presided over by the ex-FAR, and by the Interahamwe, the camps were rapidly organized into perfect replicas of the Hutu Power—same community groupings, same leaders, same rigid hierarchy, same propaganda, same violence. In this regime, the humanitarians were treated rather like the service staff at a seedy mafia-occupied hotel: they were there to provide—food, medicine, housewares, an aura of respectability.

focus on patterns of distribution of resources and should emphasize inclusiveness of opportunities and voice among groups as well as individuals. Once these local networks and associations are identified, they should be incorporated into the process of reconstruction. Even when the web of extant social capital relations is used, international actors must be wary of overloading the abilities of local staff without providing commensurate capacity-building and technical support. Assistance, whether humanitarian or development oriented, should be additive, not substitutional. Ironically, the same bonding social capital that "enables" people to survive violent conflict can become a "disabling" element for development.

2. In the transitional phase from humanitarian relief to development, *longer-term developmental actors should be more sensitive about the support of physical linkages at the expense of integrative relations.* Lack of basic infrastructure, particularly transportation, communication, power, and water supply, is a major hurdle for sustainable development. "Where a road passes, development follows right on its heels," said an old man in Cameroon (Narayan and others 2000). Transportation and communication links both increase physical and social connectedness and effect the prices obtained for crops and products. Roads, even to the next village, are seen as expanding people's options and access to services. Access to clean drinking water and to water for irrigation is frequently seen as marking the division between the nonpoor and the poor (Narayan and others 2000).

Yet in this drive to develop, community members can begin to feel disconnected from their own families and thus perceive their integrative relations to be diminishing. Globalization, while encouraging open markets and the growth of bridging networks, can worsen this condition during postconflict phases. Development efforts should try to nurture activities that help maintain integrative links in the community, uniting members of nuclear and extended families and neighbors by encouraging cross-cutting associational behavior, whether through such activities as sports and popular culture or through the ethnic makeup of local governments and enterprises.

As Figure 2 illustrates, bonding social capital and related humanitarian assistance tend to address the "legacy" of conflict (displacement, famine, disease, and death), while social and economic development that builds bridging social capital addresses

Figure 2   Toward the integration of relief and development

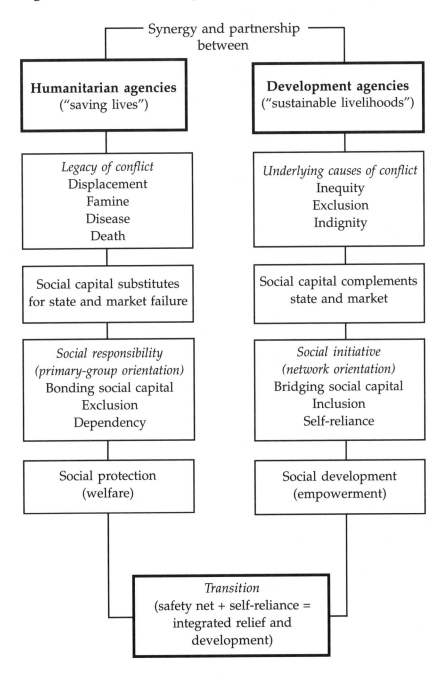

the underlying "causes" of conflict (inequity, exclusion, and indignity). A key social development task for humanitarian and development agencies is to consciously build bridging and linking (horizontal and vertical) social capital within communities and between the state and civil society when providing relief and rehabilitation that is not simply supply-driven and promotes a coping rather than change orientation.

The Brookings initiative described in Box 15 offers a promising approach to closing the gap between relief and development

---

Box 15   Bridging the gap between humanitarian relief and development

The United Nations High Commissioner for Refugees (UNHCR), the United Nations Development Programme (UNDP), and the World Bank recently initiated a program, spurred by an initiative of the Brookings Institution, to ease the discontinuity between short-term humanitarian assistance and longer-term development interventions. The transition period from humanitarian assistance and conflict to development efforts and peace is complicated by a set of socioeconomic, political, and psychological challenges within an uncertain security environment. Current responses to these challenges are inadequate because of the different approaches, institutional arrangements, and funding systems of the two types of actors. Humanitarian assistance is often unsustainable, and donors often lack interest in the transition period.

The arbitrary compartments of humanitarian activities and development do not transfer well to real-world societies, where the fragility of peace and the persistence of violence make it difficult to draw distinctions between the "conflict" and "postconflict" periods. Humanitarian operations focus on quick response and short-term planning, while development agencies are often slow and inflexible. Both tend to focus too much on mandates rather on the needs of those affected by war, and neither seems to rely on the knowledge and expertise of the other that may help improve operations. To address this gap, multilateral and bilateral institutions must become more coherent in their strategies and operations. The UNHCR, the UNDP, and the World Bank have therefore set out to establish recommendations on how to link their operations and policies to address this shortcoming. The recent joint mission to Sierra Leone, Liberia, and Guinea makes possible a grounding of mandates in the realities of the subregion. Taking a subregional perspective, its focus on such cross-border issues as refugee and arms flows, natural resources, and security concerns is bringing about synergy and improved coordination of policies and programs on the ground.

during the critical transition from war to peace. Sensitivity regarding self-reliance and social development is vital when providing relief. Relief and development should not be seen as sequential processes. Notions of a continuum are long dead. Humanitarian relief provides a window of opportunity for building bridging social capital and facilitating an environment of good governance and democratic openness. It is a vehicle when linked with development for building communication and trust across ethnic, religious, sectoral, and political lines. The integration of relief and development interventions, starting with a shared set of principles and a common assessment of local needs and capacities, is a key ingredient in closing the gaps, strengthening social capital and societal cohesion, and preventing the recurrence of violent conflict.

From Peacebuilding to Nation-Building: Designs for Sustainable Peace, Reconciliation, and Development

The challenge of nation-building remains a pressing issue for the new millennium as new states preside over old societies and unyielding social divisions. The process of decolonization continues; national elites that only recently achieved their own independence from foreign rule have to deal with dissenting communities that now demand autonomy or even independence. The task of drawing on old traditions, values, and myths to create a new nation is complex and fraught with difficulty. Yet such newly formed "imagined communities" somehow have to set aside primordial loyalties of bonded social capital manifested in religion, clan, ethnicity, and locality, to be transformed into socially cohesive, functioning nations (Shoesmith 2000). Like nation-building, social cohesion has to be built brick by brick, from the bottom up, perhaps horizontally first and then vertically. By at first overtly tackling "safe" subjects such as the community management of basic services—schools, health centers, and so on—it is possible to address the building of cross-cutting social capital by "stealth" (Khin-Sandi Lwin 2000: 3; Colletta and Nezam 1999).

Reconciliation itself is a process of rebuilding social capital. It requires the creation of political space and social relationships for peaceful engagement across and within societal cleavages be they ethnic, religious, gender, age, income, or locality, and between national and local levels.

Anticipatory thinking based on the willingness to listen and learn and to make few, if any, assumptions, is the key to success for those working in conflict-affected countries. Peacebuilding is, at its core, civil-society building. Measures of civic engagement, along with human security and government efficacy, transparency, and stability, are fundamental social capital indicators for comprehensive reconstruction. Social networks and organizations are essential assets in the portfolio of resources drawn on by the war-affected to manage risk and take advantage of opportunities. Peacebuilding involves not only economic reconstruction, or the rebuilding of physical infrastructure and economic stabilization, but also the fundamental revitalization of positive social capital and the strengthening of social cohesion. The solutions to conflict prevention lie not only in demilitarization and in jump-starting the economy, although these are important. They lie also in good governance—the rule of law, justice, and human rights—and in strengthening social capital at every level. The crucial challenge is to build societal capacity for managing diversity and preventing social capital from being transformed into an instrument of exclusion and violent conflict. This integral component of rehabilitation, reconstruction, and reconciliation can be accumulated only over years of support and nourishment. It thus requires long-term, flexible approaches that allow adaptation to interim change.

In the end, the voices of the war-affected cry out for a new kind of security, a human security devoid of oppression and fear, devoid of hunger, and rich with opportunity, that empowers them to take responsibility and decisions that impact their own lives. Resilient communities rely on all forms of responsibility and social capital: bonding primary ties for protection and survival in time of crisis; bridging links for action and development in time of hope; efficient and functional bureaucracies and transparent norms and rules; and synergistic government-community relations that allow civic engagement to thrive as the ultimate guarantor against violent conflict. Development needs to nurture and transform social capital in order to create and maintain the mechanisms and institutions necessary for strengthening social cohesion, managing diversity, preventing violent conflict, and sustaining peace and reconciliation.

Notes

1. While there is a range of definitions for civil society, we use the term to mean a network of cross-cutting relations and institutions of the people that have capacity to organize and engage in public life and decisionmaking.

2. The concept of strong and weak ties can be traced to Granovetter (1973).

3. Meas Nee (private communication, March 28, 2000) notes that Prasath has stronger social capital and social cohesion and a less marked gap between rich and poor (at a lower income level than in Prey Koh). Social divisions are more prominent in Prey Koh, where market penetration is advanced and the opportunities to escape poverty are greater.

4. The Hutu are said to comprise about 85 percent of the Rwandan population, the Tutsi roughly 14 percent, and the Twa, 1 percent. Traditionally however, these figures have been based on the number of cows owned and thus may not be accurate (Prunier 1997).

5. Many revenge killings did take place throughout the genocide and in the period immediately following, as Tutsi slaughtered Hutu in retaliation for deaths in their families. Although the exact numbers are not known, the numbers of Hutu murdered by no means match those of Tutsi killed (Prunier 1997; Des Forges 1999).

6. For a similar conclusion on social capital dynamics within militias, gangs, and guerrilla groups, see World Bank 2000: 45.

7. Certain modifications have been made in CERFE's original terminology to help assimilate CERFE's concepts to the social capital canon and facilitate comparison with the other case studies. Originally, CERFE defined civil society as the enabler of social initiative, or protective relations and risk mitigation (social responsibility, as defined here), and of social capital, or the ability to initiate economic growth (social initiative, as defined here). In this monograph, CERFE's notions of social initiative and social capital are combined to represent two differ-

ent dimensions of a more traditional concept of social capital that includes both defensive and offensive relations, more akin to the general constructs of bonding and bridging social capital. See CERFE (1998, 1999).

8. Ladino is a generic term applied to those not of Mayan descent.

9. See the Search for Common Ground Website, <www.sfcg.org>.

Annex

Learning from the Methodologies Employed: Measuring Social Capital within a Context of Violent Conflict

Using Woolcock's four dimensions of social capital, comparative analysis of the definitions and indicators of social capital employed by the country studies reveals the advantages and disadvantages of each method and suggests how other external research may have furthered understanding. Such a review also illustrates the studies' contributions to the conceptualization, assessment, and measurement of social capital, illuminates areas of omission, and helps specify and focus potential interventions for directly affecting different dimensions of social capital in the processes of reconciliation and reconstruction of war-torn societies.

The definitions and indicators of social capital used in the Cambodia and Rwanda studies allowed an in-depth look at two basic dimensions of social capital: integration and linkages. The Cambodian study focused on community events, informal networks, associations, and village leadership, which helped illustrate the matrix of social relations within Prasath and Prey Koh. Links with the government and with external agencies were briefly covered, revealing the nature of vertical relations and, to a much lesser degree, the organizational integrity of the state and its synergistic relations with communities. The study in Rwanda primarily focused on integration within the commune.

Various aspects of intracommunal relations were examined, such as exchange, the presence of associations and groups, intermarriage and extended family relations, conflict-resolution mechanisms, trust, and collective responsibility toward vulnerable groups. Intercommunity ties, or linkages, were examined in terms of exchange, intermarriage, and cooperation between neighboring communes. Vertical relations with the local administration were also assessed, shedding some light on the levels of synergy in Rwanda, and the analysis of the conflict revealed the state's lack of organizational integrity.

The paradigm employed by CERFE in Guatemala and Somalia also facilitated the analysis of both integration and linkages. Social responsibility, or how well civil society can protect people from risk and adversity, was examined along with civil society's social initiative, or potential to have a positive effect on economic development and growth. This two-pronged approach to analyzing the capacity of civil society encompassed both bonding and bridging social capital, within and between communities. In its quest to lump all social capital together under the rubric of civil society, however, the CERFE model largely ignored the importance of bonding social capital manifested in kinship and informal networks and groups, notably indigenous groups in Guatemala and clan structures in Somalia.

Although the four studies revealed much about the micro aspects of social capital, they were only able to foreshadow the macro issues disclosed in the notions of state and market penetration. Overall, the models used in all the case studies did not allow for sufficient gathering of data on vertical elements of social capital related to state organizational integrity or synergy. The Rwandan and Cambodian studies tangentially covered facets of synergy and organizational integrity, but mainly through their analyses of conflict. By illuminating the capacity and function of civil society, the CERFE model, although it did not focus on organizational integrity or synergy per se, did shed light on these two macro social capital dimensions. When combined with a broader examination of government roles and abilities and of how the government relates to the community in defining and fulfilling these roles, CERFE's findings helped illustrate how civil society operated in conjunction with the state by either substituting for or complementing government action.

The balance between the four dimensions of social capital—integration, linkages, organizational integrity, and synergy—is critical, for, according to Woolcock, such balance produces the most fertile ground for stability and sustainable social and economic development and growth. This balance is the essence of societal cohesion. A lapse in any one dimension does not necessarily prevent socioeconomic development, but it could mean that growth is hampered. Consequently, efforts to nurture social capital and hence promote social and economic advances must consider each of the four dimensions of vertical and horizontal social capital. In order to capture the full impact of social capital formation on social cohesiveness, future studies should incorporate a more holistic analysis to ensure that each dimension is addressed. This broadening of conceptual analysis should, however, be accompanied by a specific definition of social capital and clear and precise indicators so as not to increase vagueness and ambiguity along with scope.

Strengths and Weaknesses of the Survey Methodologies

The methodologies employed in the studies have their strengths and weaknesses (see Table 10 for an outline of the survey methods). The Cambodian analysis used quantitative data to establish demographic background information on the communities and participatory qualitative research to examine more substantive social capital issues. Participants were questioned through surveys and in individual and group exercises that included mapping, diagram, and ranking exercises. The use of a combination of methods to gather data enabled the triangulation of findings. As a result, the final report presented a clear and detailed description of social capital and its relation to conflict in Prey Koh and Prasath, while integrating the participants' perceptions.

The Rwanda study implemented a qualitative survey and strove to integrate participants' perspectives on the concepts, definitions, and indicators of social capital and conflict. The

Table 10 Comparison of the field surveys

	Cambodia	Rwanda	Guatemala and Somalia
Literature review	June–September 1998	June–September 1998	February–July 1998
Field staff	Predominantly local; three men and two women; led by external international consultant.	Local, equally divided between men and women; overseen by the World Bank's Post-Conflict Unit and the World Bank Resident Mission.	Local; staff led by international NGO (CERFE) with extensive field presence in each country.
Fieldwork	September 1998–February 1999. Two surveys: one to establish baseline socioeconomic information (all households—130 in Prasath and 114 in Prey Koh), and a second to investigate social capital factors (about 30 percent of households, randomly selected—39 in Prasath and 34 in Prey Koh). Further qualitative data gathered through village stays and participant observation (12 weeks); participatory group exercises such as mapping, resource flow analysis, wealth	October 1998–May 1999. Household surveys covering 1.5 percent of households, randomly selected, in three sectors of each commune (114 households in Giti and 144 households in Shyanda). Each household contained five people, on average; Giti has a population of 48,000 and Shyanda a population of 39,000. The survey structure was based on findings in the initial literature review and three weeks of participant observation in each commune. Data analysis from the surveys is still in process. Focus group and key informant interviews in each commune. Focus	September 1998–February 1999. The first phase of field research was designed to identify those socially responsible collective actors (organizations) that make up civil society in each study town: • Hargeisa (Somalia): 85 • Boroma (Somalia): 44 • Nebaj (Guatemala): 51 • Puerto Barrios (Guatemala): 50 Interviews were conducted with key persons, local leaders, and civil servants. Hargeisa has a population of 295,000 (141 civil society groups) and Boroma, 64,000 (63 civil society groups). Puerto

(Table continues on next page.)

Table 10 *(continued)*

	Cambodia	Rwanda	Guatemala and Somalia
	ranking, and trend analysis; and individual and group semistructured interviews.	groups contained 5 to 15 participants and targeted mixed groups, widows, orphans, politicians, intellectuals, associations, and business people. Key informants were chosen from the focus groups to elaborate on specific details. Interview guides for both group and individual interviews were derived from initial survey findings.	Barrios has a population of 82,000 (170 civil society groups), and Nebaj has a population of 55,000 (187 civil society groups). The second phase focused on the quality of leadership in a selected number of organizations; 84 leaders in both countries were interviewed. In the third phase, 20 organizations in Guatemala and 21 in Somalia were studied in depth. A total of 41 organization leaders, 52 key persons, and 94 citizens was questioned.
Con-straints	Difficulties stemmed from the time elapsed since the pre-conflict period more than 30 years ago. Few people were old enough to recall what day-to-day existence was like, and memories had faded.	The sensitivity of the topic and the recentness of the war meant that the subject had to be approached slowly and indirectly. After the field team gained the trust of communal members, respondents freely discussed their conflict experiences.	The complexity of the model utilized and the long duration of conflict in each country made it difficult to get a picture of the changes in the variables over time.

research was participatory and was led by local consultants. It consequently yielded a very thick description of social capital within the communes from the participants' point of view without much contamination by external factors. It did not, however, supply much quantitative data to facilitate analysis and cross-country comparison.

The approach taken in Guatemala and Somalia yielded a large amount of quantifiable data but sparse qualitative information. To facilitate comparison of the two cases, the survey used set definitions of social capital and conflict as provided by external researchers. The study did not examine the presence and interactions of social capital and conflict over time and therefore provided only a snapshot of the current state of civil society in each country. Although it was difficult to ascertain how participants viewed the issues under scrutiny, as there is little qualitative explanatory power in the methodology, the four-country comparative workshop was extremely useful in enhancing the explanatory power for research findings and assessing the methodologies themselves.

Lessons for Future Research

Two of the three main constraints on the four studies—the sensitivity of the subject and the time elapsed since the preconflict period—are constant. Another major limitation, the time and resources allotted for the research, can be altered. Future studies should allow more time for field research, especially in view of the sensitivity of the topic. As is often the case, budgets are limiting factors in the scope and scale of field inquiry. The primary constraint on comparative analysis of the four case studies is the difference in the approaches utilized in the studies. Guatemala and Somalia employed the same methodology, but it differed somewhat from those used in Cambodia and Rwanda, which also differed from each other. Factors relating to methodology, such as the time allotted to desk and field research and the size, qualifications, and composition of field teams, also varied. Finally, some cases relied on quantitative data, while others focused heavily on qualitative data.

As a preliminary exercise in research on the relation between social capital, social cohesion, and violent conflict, the project yielded some recommendations for future studies. They include the following:

- Employ the same definitions and indicators of social capital and conflict in each case. In the pretest, a few country-specific indicators may be added to deepen the analysis, but the use of an original set of indicators applied to each case will allow a firmer comparison and generalization of findings.
- Combine surveys with participatory methods such as individual and group exercises using diagram, ranking, and mapping exercises, thus making triangulation possible.
- Creatively integrate quantitative and qualitative data. Use initial qualitative data to design a quantitative survey. The results can then be reaffirmed through subsequent qualitative research.
- Match the model of social capital employed to the desired outcomes. For instance, if the goal is to produce recommendations for government action, the social capital paradigm should include aspects of organizational integrity and synergy, with a focus of all four dimensions on the degree of social cohesiveness and subsequent management of conflict.

The variation in case study methods adds to the difficulty of making quantitative comparisons across data sets. On the positive side, the qualitative comparative analysis is rich in insights, generating a host of observations and recommendations for future policy and programmatic actions designed to strengthen social capital as a key ingredient in reconciliation, relief, reconstruction, and development.

Bibliography

Adam, Hussein, and Richard Ford, with Ali Jimale Ahmed, Abdinasir Osman Isse, Nur Weheliye, and David Smock. 1998. *Removing Barricades in Somalia: Options for Peace and Rehabilitation.* Peaceworks 24. Washington, D.C.: United States Institute of Peace.

Becker, Elizabeth. 1998. *When the War Was Over: Cambodia and the Khmer Rouge Revolution.* New York: Public Affairs.

Berdal, Mats, and David Malone. 2000. *Greed and Grievance: Economic Agendas in Civil Wars.* Boulder, Colo.: Lynne Rienner.

Berger, Peter L., ed. 1998. *The Limits of Social Cohesion: Conflict and Mediation in Pluralistic Societies.* Boulder, Colo.: Westview Press.

Berkeley, Bill. 1998. "Judgement Day." *The Washington Post Magazine* (October 11): 10–15, 25–29.

Berkman, Lisa F., and Ichiro Kawachi, eds. 2000. *Social Epidemiology.* New York: Oxford University Press.

Bit, Seanglim, ed. 1991. *The Warrior Heritage: A Psychological Perspective of Cambodian Trauma.* El Cerrito, Calif.: Seanglim Bit.

Cambodia, Kingdom of, Ministry of Planning. 1999. *Cambodia Human Development Report 1999: Village Economy and Development.* Phnom Penh.

Carnegie Commission on Preventing Deadly Conflict. 1997. *Preventing Deadly Conflict: Executive Summary of the Final Report.* New York: Carnegie Corporation of New York.

CERFE. 1998. "The Depletion and Restoration of Social Capital in War-Torn Societies: Phase 2—Somalia and Guatemala. First Progress Report." Study conducted for the World Bank.

————. 1999. "Civil Society, Social Initiative and Social Capital in Somalia and Guatemala. Final Report." Study conducted for the
World Bank.

Chandler, David. 1992. *Brother Number One: A Political Biography of Pol
Pot*. Boulder, Colo.: Westview Press.

Coleman, James S. 1988. "Social Capital in the Creation of Human
Capital." *American Journal of Sociology* 94 (Supplement): S95–S120.

Colletta, Nat J., and Markus Kostner. 2000. "Reforming Development
Cooperation: From Reconstruction to Prevention." *Forum*: Special
Issue on War, Money, and Survival (February): 96–99. International
Committee of the Red Cross: Geneva.

Colletta, Nat J., and Taies Nezam. 1999. "From Reconstruction to Reconciliation: The Nature of War Determines the Nature of Peace."
Development Outreach 1 (2): 5–8.

Collier, Paul. 1998. "Social Capital and Poverty." Social Capital Initiative Working Paper 4. Economically and Socially Sustainable Development Network, World Bank, Washington, D.C. Available at
<http://www.worldbank.org/poverty/scapital/wkrppr>.

Collier, Paul, and Anke Hoeffler. 1998. "On Economic Causes of Civil
War." *Oxford Economic Papers* 50 (October): 563–73.

————. 1999. "Justice-Seeking and Loot-Seeking in Civil War." World
Bank, Washington, D.C. Available at <http://www.worldbank.org/
research/conflict/papers/justice.htm>.

Costello, Patrick. 1995. "Guatemala. Displacement, Return and the Peace
Process." Writenet (U.K.). Available at <http://www.unhcr.ch/
refworld/country/writenet/wrigtm.htm>.

Cuny, Frederick C. 1994. *Disasters and Development*. Dallas: Intertect
Press.

Deacon, Robert. 2000. "Globalization and Social Policy: The Threat of
Equitable Welfare." Occasional Paper No. 5, March 2000. Geneva:
United Nations Research Institute Social Development.

Des Forges, Alison. 1999. *"Leave None to Tell the Story": Genocide in
Rwanda*. New York: Human Rights Watch; Paris: International Fed-
eration of Human Rights.

Easterly, William. 1999. "Life during Growth: International Evidence
on Quality of Life and Per Capita Income." Policy Research Working Paper 2110. Macroeconomics and Growth, Development Research Group, World Bank, Washington, D.C.

————. 2000a. "Can Institutions Resolve Ethnic Conflict?" Development Economics Vice Presidency, World Bank, Washington, D.C.
Available at <http://www.worldbank.org/html/prdmg/
grthweb/institutions.htm>.

———. 2000b. "The Middle Class Consensus and Economic Development." Development Economics Vice Presidency, World Bank, Washington, D.C. Available at <http://www.worldbank.org/html/prdmg/grthweb/midclass.htm>.

Ebihara, May M., Carol A. Morland, and Judy Ledgerwood, eds. 1994. *Cambodian Culture since 1975: Homeland and Exile*. Ithaca, N.Y.: Cornell University Press.

Faulder, Dominic. 2000. "A State of Injustice: Violence and Impunity Are Alive and Well." *Asia Week* (March 3).

Fedderke, Johannes, and Robert Klitgaard. 1998. "Economic Growth and Social Indicators: An Exploratory Analysis." *Economic Development and Cultural Change* 46 (3): 455–89.

Fukuyama, Francis. 1995. *Trust: The Social Values and the Creation of Prosperity*. New York: Free Press.

Galtung, Johan. 1996. *Peace by Peaceful Means: Peace and Conflict, Development and Civilization*. International Peace Research Institute, Oslo. Thousand Oaks, Calif.: Sage Publications.

Gissinger, Ranveig, and Nils Petter Gleditch. 1999. "Globalization and Conflict: Welfare, Distribution, and Political Unrest." *Journal of World Systems Research* 5: 274–300.

Gittell, Ross, and Avis Vidal. 1998. *Community Organizing: Building Social Capital as a Development Strategy*. Thousand Oaks, Calif.: Sage Publications.

Goodhand, Jonathan, and David Hulme. 1999. "NGOs and Peacebuilding in Complex Political Emergencies: An Introduction." Working Paper No. 1. University of Manchester and INTRAC.

Gourevitch, Philip. 1998. *We Wish to Inform You That Tomorrow We Will Be Killed with Our Families*. New York: Farrar, Straus and Giroux.

Granovetter, Mark S. 1973. "The Strength of Weak Ties." *American Journal of Sociology* 78: 1360–80.

Grootaert, Christiaan. 1998. "Social Capital: The Missing Link?" Social Capital Initiative Working Paper 3. Environmentally and Socially Sustainable Development Network. World Bank, Washington, D.C. Available at <http://www.worldbank.org/poverty/scapital/wkrppr>.

Gurr, Ted Robert. Forthcoming. *Peoples versus States*. Washington, D.C.: United States Institute of Peace Press.

Humphreys, Bebbington, Denise, and Arelis Gomez. 2000. "Rebuilding Social Capital in Postconflict Regions: Women's Village Banking in Ayacucho, Peru, and in Highland Guatemala." Paper presented at meeting of the Latin American Studies Association, Miami, March 16.

Kawachi, Ichiro, and Lisa F. Berkman. 2000. "Social Cohesion, Social Capital, and Health." In Lisa F. Berkman and Ichiro Kawachi, eds., *Social Epidemiology.* New York: Oxford University Press.

Khin-Sandi Lwin. 2000. "Conflict Management: Experiences of International and Regional Organizations." Paper presented at the Asian Development Bank–World Bank Regional Consultation on "Social Cohesion and Conflict Management," Manila, March 16–17.

Kostner, Markus, Taies Nezam, and Colin Scott. 1997. "From Civil War to Civil Society: The Transition from War to Peace in Guatemala and Liberia." Post-Conflict Unit, World Bank, Washington, D.C.

Krishnamurthy, Veena. 1999. "The Impact of Armed Conflict on Social Capital: A Study of Two Villages in Cambodia." Study conducted for the World Bank by Social Services of Cambodia. Social Services of Cambodia: Phnom Penh.

Lemarchand, René. 1970. *Burundi and Rwanda.* New York: Praeger.

Martin, Keith. 1996a. "New Measures in Conflict Prevention." *Canadian Foreign Policy / La Politique étrangère du Canada* 4 (1): 139–43.

———. 1996b. "Rethinking Foreign Policy: From Managing to Preventing Conflict." *Policy Options / Politiques* 17 (3, April): 30–34.

Menkhaus, Ken. 1998. "Somalia: Political Order in a Stateless Society." *Current History* (May): 220–33.

Nafizer, E. W., F. Steward, and R. Vayrynen, eds. 2000. *The Origin of Humanitarian Emergencies in the Third World.* New York: Oxford University Press.

Narayan, Deepa. 1999. "Bonds and Bridges: Social Capital and Poverty." Policy Research Working Paper 2167. Poverty Division, Poverty Reduction and Economic Management Network, World Bank, Washington, D.C.

Narayan, Deepa, Raj Patel, Kai Schafft, Anne Rademacher, Sarah Koch-Schulte, Robert Chambers, Meera Shah, and Patti Petesch. 2000. *Voices of the Poor.* 3 vols. New York: Oxford University Press.

Nathan, Laurie. 1998. "Crisis Resolution and Conflict Management in Africa." Paper commissioned for a conference on "The Nexus between Economic Management and Civil Society in Countries Emerging from War in the SADC Region," sponsored by the Centre for Conflict Resolution and the World Bank Post-Conflict Unit, Cape Town, South Africa, October 11–13.

Nee, Meas. 1995. "Towards Restoring Life: Cambodian Villages. Told by Meas Nee; with Joan Healy as Listener and Scribe." Overseas Service Bureau, Melbourne, Australia.

———. 2000. "Conflict and Peace in Cambodia: Some Lessons Learnt." Paper presented at Asian Development Bank–World Bank Regional Consultation on "Social Cohesion and Conflict Management," Manila, March 16–17.

Newbury, Catharine. 1988. *The Cohesion of Oppression: Clientship and Ethnicity in Rwanda 1860–1960*. New York: Columbia University Press.

North, Douglas C. 1990. *Institutions, Institutional Change, and Economic Performance*. New York: Cambridge University Press.

Olson, Mancur. 1982. *The Rise and Decline of Nations: Economic Growth, Stagflation, and Social Rigidities*. New Haven, Conn.: Yale University Press.

Prendergast, John, and Matt Bryden. 1999. "War and Peace in Somalia and Somaliland: A Report of the Center for the Strategic Initiatives of Women." Center for the Strategic Initiatives of Women, Washington, D.C.

Prunier, Gérard. 1997. *The Rwanda Crisis: History of a Genocide*. New York: Columbia University Press.

Putnam, Robert D. 1993. "The Prosperous Community: Social Capital and Public Life." *American Prospect* 13: 35–42.

Reno, William. 1998. *Warlord Politics and African States*. Boulder, Colo.: Lynne Rienner.

Richards, Paul. 1995. *Fighting for the Rain Forest: War, Youth and Resources in Sierra Leone*. London: James Currey.

Rodriguez, Melania P. 1977. "Social Capital in Developing Societies: Reconsidering the Links between Civil Agency, Economy and the State in the Development Process." Working Paper. Institute of Social Studies, The Hague.

Rodrik, Dani. 1999a. *The New Global Economy and Developing Countries: Making Openness Work*. Baltimore, Md.: Johns Hopkins University Press.

———. 1999b. "Where Did All the Growth Go? External Shocks, Social Conflict, and Growth Collapses." *Journal of Economic Growth* 4 (4, December): 385–412.

Sen, Amartya. 1999. *Development as Freedom*. New York: Knopf.

Shah, Anwar. 1998. "Balance and Responsiveness: Lessons about Decentralization." World Bank, Operations Evaluation Department, Washington, D.C.

Shoesmith, Dennis. 2000. "Implementing Autonomy: Laws, Religion, and Culture." Paper presented at conference on "Autonomy and Democracy in Asia and the Pacific," Darwin, Australia, March 1–3.

Smith, Gordon, and Moises Naim. 2000. *Altered States: Globalization, Sovereignty and Governance*. Ottawa: International Development Research Centre.

Sollenberg, Margareta, ed. 1998. "States in Armed Conflict 1998." Report 54. Department of Peace and Conflict Research, Uppsala University, Sweden.

Story, Andy. 1998. "Structural Adjustment and Ethnicity: A Framework for Analysis and a Case Study of Rwanda." World Bank, Washington, D.C. Processed.

Uphoff, Norman. 2000. "Understanding Social Capital: Learning from the Analysis and Experience of Participation." In Partha Dasgupta and Ismail Serageldin, eds. *Social Capital: A Multifaceted Perspective*, 215–52. Sociological Perspectives on Development series. Washington, D.C.: World Bank.

Uvin, Peter. 1998. *Aiding Violence: The Development Enterprise in Rwanda*. West Hartford, Conn.: Kumarian Press.

van de Put, Willem. 1997. "Community Mental Health Program. Facts and Thoughts on the First Years: 1 February 1995–1 October 1996." Transcultural Psychosocial Organization (Amsterdam), Phnom Penh.

Vijghen, John, and others. 1966. "Customs of Patronage and Community Development in a Cambodian Village." Cambodia Researchers for Development, Institute for Social Research and Training, Phnom Penh.

Wallensteen, Peter, and Margareta Sollenberg. 1996. "Armed Conflict, Conflict Termination, and Peace Agreements 1989–96." *Journal of Peace Research* 33 (3, August): 339–58.

Woolcock, Michael. 1998. "Social Capital and Economic Development: Towards a Theoretical Synthesis and Policy Framework." *Theory and Society* 27 (2): 151–208.

World Bank. 1998. "Project Appraisal Document on a Proposed Learning and Innovation Credit in the Amount of SDR 3.7 Million (US$5.0 Million) to the Rwandese Republic for a Community Reintegration and Development Project." Country Department 9 and Human Development 4, Africa Region, Washington, D.C.

————. 1999. "Project Appraisal Document on a Proposed Learning and Innovation Credit in the Amount of SDR 3.6 Million Equivalent to the Kingdom of Cambodia for a Northeast Village Development Project, April 30, 1999." Rural Development and Natural Resources Sector Unit and East Asia and Pacific Region, Washington, D.C.

———. 2000. *Violence in Colombia: Building Sustainable Peace and Social Capital.* A World Bank Country Study. Washington, D.C.

———. 2000. *World Development Report 2000.* Washington, D.C.

Zartman, I. William, and Victor A. Kremenyuk, eds. 1995. *Cooperative Security: Reducing Third World Wars.* Syracuse Studies on Peace and Conflict Resolution. Syracuse, N.Y.: Syracuse University Press.